Look What's on the Bench

Look What's on the Bench

by

Eric Crowther

Published by

Barry Rose Publishers

Chichester

England

ISBN 1 872328 18 0
First Published 1992

Published by Barry Rose Publishers Ltd
Chichester, England

DEDICATION

To Galina from the Ukraine,
who helped me with reading the proofs
Eric Crowther

Foreword

London is Eric Crowther's village, and, as a London Stipendiary Magistrate, his court was, for him, its parish pump. In it he presided for many years over the foibles and failings of his fellow Londoners. He did so with wisdom, dressed-down as common sense, and wry humour or compassion when appropriate.

I met him first over thirty years ago when he was a young barrister giving free legal advice on Wednesday evenings at Toynbee Hall Legal Advice Centre in London's East End. His understanding of and genuine interest in other people's problems, and his readiness to support them against authority when necessary, marked him out as a fine advocate. They were qualities which equally fitted him for the Bench, and they shine through this account of his time as a "Stipe".

This is a compelling read for those who have practised in the London Metropolitan Magistrates' Courts and for those who have never seen the inside of a court. In its modest way it is a piece of social history, engagingly written, and a fitting sequel to his highly successful story of his life at the Bar, "Last in the List".

Robin Auld,
Royal Courts of Justice,
Strand,
London, WC2.

12 November, 1991

Non-Introduction

New Year's Eve 1988 was a remarkable day for me. A radio programme proclaimed the earlier part of my autobiography *Last in the List* as "Book of the Year" – I should keep a sense of proportion by adding that the channel was L.B.C.! – and I received two letters from professional writers who had been given *Last in the List* as Christmas presents. One was a former pupil of mine who, while still young, gave up his wig to pursue a career with his pen; the other, whom I have never met, was the distinguished author and broadcaster C.H. Rolph. Both condemned my "long" and "boring" introduction. Mr Rolph wrote: "It was so tedious that it almost put me off reading the rest of the book, which would have been a pity, because I found it absolutely fascinating. Never make such a mistake again!" (My former pupil was less kind.)

That is why, dear Reader, this latest and last book of mine is offered with only a brief non-introduction.

Contents

Chapter 1

The Jailors

The cells at Horseferry Road are four floors down from the main Courts. As the defendant clambered laboriously up the steps her screams of protest got louder, and it was no surprise to realize, as I looked into my register, that the charge was one of criminal damage by breaking a window of a police station. Eventually the dock at Court Number One at Horseferry Road was occupied by a gnome-like crone, who peered over the rails and, regarding me disapprovingly, exclaimed: "Cor! Look what's on the Bench! They really are scraping the bottom of the barrel, aren't they?"

However, I was grateful to her, for she was to provide the title of the second part of my autobiography, and I wanted it to include the word "Bench" to distinguish this part from *Last in the List*, in which I attempted to describe life at the Bar. I had intended to call this book "He's on the Bench!" in honour of Wally, for many years our jailor at West London Court. Wally was a kind of Gilbert and Sullivan policeman, forever rushing hither and thither, sliding rather than running, his slides usually ending in a collision with the dock or the witness box, and occasionally a collapse on the floor.

The Court was never ready to start on time when Wally was jailor, so, in order to precipitate matters I would sometimes enter Court unannounced and take my seat. Wally would come slithering back from the cell area and, viewing me with horror, would yell down to his colleague in charge of the prisoners: "He's on the Bench!"

He was not very effective and it was perhaps fortunate that it was not he but Jock who was on duty when my predecessor, dear old Alan

Stevenson, was shot at from the dock by a nasty American called Greenberg, who, when Alan refused him bail, glanced around to the public gallery, whence his German girlfriend threw a revolver to him. His first shot narrowly missed Alan, but the second landed in the ceiling of the Court, because by now Jock had intervened and overpowered the gunman.

Wally would have been just as brave, but I doubt if he would have got there quite so quickly. But he was conscientious and kind and a good policeman and we missed him a lot when eventually he was transferred to fresh fields and pastures new.

After the second shot Alan Stevenson, who was a little deaf, looked up and said: "Quiet please. There's too much noise in Court. Call the next case." He was greatly praised for his coolness under fire, but confessed to me that he had not realized that he had been shot at until he was told this during the luncheon adjournment. The sentence of five years that Greenberg got at the Old Bailey for attempted murder might have been sufficient if the intended victim had been some of my colleagues, but was certainly not enough when Alan was the target.

One of the people that Wally and Jock had to guide almost daily to the dock was the late, lamented Paddy Nolan, one of the great characters of West London. Nearly all Paddy's offences were drink-related: drunk, drunk and disorderly, threatening behaviour, assault on police, etc. In the morning he was invariably courteous and contrite, and he usually got away with light sentences. One day he appeared before me on an unusual charge. "Patrick Nolan," intoned the clerk, "you are charged with stealing a bottle of milk to the value of seven and a half pence. How do you plead?"

"Not guilty," Paddy pronounced firmly, adding for good measure: "What would I be wanting with a bottle of milk?" "Well, I can't deal with the case today," I sighed. "It will have to go over for a week for the matter to be tried." (The waiting time in Courts has increased in the last 15 years almost as much as the price of a bottle of milk.) "I object to bail, Your Worships," intervened the young police officer (he addressed me in the plural as policemen often do) "on the ground that Mr Nolan is of

No Fixed Abode."

Paddy, already incensed by the insulting nature of the charge, fairly bristled with anger: "What does he mean – No Fixed Abode?" he demanded. "I sleep every night on Shepherds Bush Green. That's where the police arrest me every night of me life. Why, you saw me there yourself, Mr Crowther, only last Friday when you were returning home late from –" "Mr Nolan," I interjected in an attempt to get the case back to more relevant issues. "If I grant you bail how can I be sure that you'll turn up a week today?" Mr Nolan looked me straight in the eye: "Of course I'll turn up if I promise to. I'm a man of my convictions." I granted him bail; he appeared the next week and was acquitted.

It was to the great credit of the local police that when Paddy died, at the age of 34, of cirrhosis of the liver, many of the officers whom he had assaulted in his drunken rages attended his funeral, after which a wreath was laid on his grave on behalf of "Paddy's friends in the Metropolitan Police". These included the jailors who had so often guided Paddy's unsteady steps towards the dock.

Jailors are a rather special breed of men. They are usually middle-aged or elderly police officers who have not risen above the rank of constable, although a few are sergeants. They vary in appearance and temperament, of course, just as do barristers and magistrates, but during nearly 40 years in the law I have come across very few of them that I disliked.

Jock, at West London, who so bravely saved Alan Stevenson's life, was not favourably disposed towards young people and could not abide drug addicts. This latter group, anxious to get to their next "fix", are prone to go on arguing after they have been sentenced, and Jock would deal with this situation by shouting firmly: "This way"; and if they disobeyed his direction, he would drag them with considerable force from the dock. I could not dissuade him from this habit which, to use the former Chief Metropolitan Magistrate Sir Frank Milton's famous expression, was "bad for our image".

Provided that the defendant will finish talking or protesting within a reasonable time (a few minutes) I am in favour of letting him have his say, but I could not convince Jock of the rectitude of this policy. Once when I thought he had used "more force than was reasonably necessary" I got on to the Commander that afternoon and he asked: "Do you want him moved?" I had not expected such a question, but my frank reply was "Yes", and, to my amazement, next day Jock had been moved to a position in charge of the Sports Section of the Metropolitan Police, for which his physical prowess well suited him.

Never before or since have I felt the exercise of such instant power, but I was happy to see Jock go, although I would have been glad to have had him around had there been another Greenberg in the dock, and I must say in fairness that he was always very kind to pathetic old ladies accused of shoplifting.

The senior jailor at Marlborough Street some years ago was not a very sympathetic personality. At about 9.30 a.m. he received a telephone call at the Court and a lady was speaking: "I'm calling from Liverpool. I'm sorry, but my boy's going to be late for Court this morning. He's not been at all well this week-end."

"Well," said the jailor, rather harshly. "He'd better get his skates on. Our Magistrate's very bad-tempered and he doesn't have much patience with people who arrive late at Court."

"But you don't understand," said the plaintive voice on the other end of the phone. "My boy *is* the Magistrate." (Clyde Wilson, who was a bachelor, used to visit his elderly mother in Liverpool most week-ends).

I have known other jailors who have been cynical and ironic, but the vast majority are kindly men. One at my last Court we all called "the Bishop", for he moved with the stately dignity appropriate to episcopal office. They are worldly-wise, or at least Court-wise, and it is a foolish young barrister who displays arrogance to the jailor when he wants to "get on early", for he will discover that his rudeness usually leads to his being "last on the list". He should realize that he is dealing with one of the most influential and knowledgeable people in the Court.

Often the official of the Crown Prosecution Service will say, on a plea of guilty: "There's nothing known about the defendant, sir. He's a man of good character," and the smile will disappear from the defendant's face as the jailor quietly adds: "He was here the day before yesterday, sir. It was his fourteenth appearance this year. I can't of course speak for other Courts."

At Thames when I was there one of our jailors was Mr Bates, a veritable "gentleman's gentleman". It was touching to see him directing the drunks gently into the dock with soft words like: "This way, sir, if you please. And would you kindly remain standing until the learned Magistrate says you may be seated?" He might equally have been escorting them into the lift at Claridges!

Another jailor of my time at Thames was of a rougher disposition. A defendant appeared in the dock and was asked by the Clerk: "Were you drunk last night?" "Well, I'd had one or two," replied the defendant. "Yes, but were you drunk?" "I had had a drink, I must admit." "But were you drunk?" "Well, it's my legs, isn't it?" At that point the jailor could stand it no longer, and went over and shook the defendant. "You were drunk, weren't you?" he bellowed. "Yes," admitted the defendant, and an unequivocal plea was entered.

The same jailor was in Court when a rather pathetic man pleaded guilty to theft. "What is your occupation?" I asked, seeking to assess the appropriate level of fine. The defendant was not only feeble; he was also rather deaf. "I've got seven children," he replied, sadly but irrelevantly. The jailor moved over to him menacingly: "The Magistrate wants to know what you do in the daytime," he demanded.

Chapter 2

Early Crises

The transition from Bar to Bench, for which I had so much longed, was not without its problems. I had asked Harold Sturge, a very experienced Metropolitan Magistrate before whom I had frequently appeared and who had often spoken at my Law Group at the British Council, to act as one of my referees. He had refused, saying that he did not know me well enough. It was ironical that it was him whom I succeeded; even more so that in retirement he should ask me to use my influence to secure an appointment for him as a Deputy.

The bureaucracy involved in judicial appointments was much less apparent 20 years ago than it is now, when I believe that the applicant is asked how much tobacco, alcohol, coffee and tea he consumes. (I should avoid the question about alcohol, and be failed on tea!) Even so, the Lord Chancellor's Office required a certificate from one's own regular doctor about one's physical fitness before one took up the post, so I repaired to my general practitioner for this purpose.

Dr Finlay (not his real name), our National Health Service representative, was a dour Scot. He was the only medical person I have ever known who examined two patients simultaneously (with a curtain in between): it saved time. Once when Elke (my wife) was away I went to dine in a restaurant and seeing him sitting alone at a table, I went to join him. "Would you mind sitting elsewhere?" he asked. "I don't mix socially with patients."

His receptionists were as unfriendly as he:

"What's wrong with you?" asked the girl.

"Nothing," I replied. "I need a certificate to say that I am fit."

"Don't waste our time," she admonished. "The doctor is here to deal with sick people, not those who are well."

"I need it for my appointment as a Magistrate. I must have it," I protested.

"Go away," she ordered. "Otherwise I will call the police."

"I demand to see the doctor," I said. "Otherwise I will complain to the Regional Health Authority."

"But you are not ill."

"I am becoming ill because of you. I have a right to see the doctor."

She disappeared for a few minutes and then returned.

"The doctor refuses to see you," she asserted triumphantly.

"Then I shall wait here until the end of his surgery," I insisted.

"He says I should call the police."

"Do."

So I waited, and about an hour and a half later the doctor emerged and without a word handed me a note signed by him which read: "Mr Eric Crowther is fit to be a Magistrate."

Sir Thomas Skyrme, Secretary of Commissions, complained that it was unusually laconic, but when I explained the situation, accepted it, to my considerable relief.

A certain dissatisfaction that I had long felt with Dr Finlay effervesced through this incident into a desire that my family and I should leave his list. But it was not so easy. A few months earlier an insurance company had required of me a medical examination by another local doctor, who had seemed very pleasant, but when I approached him, Dr Scrivener said: "No. I have always found that those who want to change from other doctors are trouble-makers." However, a few months later, his secretary telephoned to say that he was taking in a partner who would need patients, and we could go on his list if we wished.

This young man left soon, and then we were transferred to the sole practice of Dr Scrivener, who looked after us well and became a personal friend. When he retired about four years ago his practice was transferred to Dr Wilkes, whom I had known as a very fair and efficient young police surgeon, and so now our medical affairs are looked after by a practitioner who combines competence with charm, and we feel happy with this aspect of the National Health Service. But I think that the Government was right recently to permit the patient freedom to change his medical practitioner; freedom to find one who is willing to write: "This patient is well."

Not long after my appointment I needed a good doctor. In September, 1968, I developed a bad cold. It got worse, but I did not want to go sick a month or so after the start of my judicial career, so I carried on working. This was unwise. Even more foolish was my decision to accompany Elke and our children to the middle of Germany for the wedding of Elke's brother, Ludwig, in Hannoversch. München. But I did not want to miss this great occasion; nor did I want Elke to be the only driver on that 700-mile journey.

So we set off for the night boat at the beginning of November. There was black fog in the Channel: ("Continent cut off from Britain" as the famous Chauvinistic headline in the *Daily Express* once said) and then we struggled through ice and fog over Belgium into Germany where, in the middle of the night, I gave up driving, got out of our car, and found myself coughing up lots of blood. I never got to the wedding. A fashionable young German doctor in Elke's home town laughingly diagnosed: "There's nothing wrong with you that a couple of bottles of red wine won't put right," and he charged me many marks for this advice and threatened to return the next day. It was the only time I recall that I have not felt like imbibing red wine and I decided that I was really ill and would prefer to return to the care of the British National Health Service, so I flew back to London, alone, next day.

From my bed I phoned Dr Finlay. He refused to come to see me. I had been a source of trouble to him when I was well, even attempting to leave his list, so why should he bother with me when I was ill? I lay in bed, sweating and feeling that I was going to die. Alone at home I tried to think of all the doctors that, as a barrister, I had represented (mostly on drunken driving charges . . .)

There was a bad flu epidemic on at the time and all were too busy with their own patients to come to me. Then after three days of eating nothing and sweating all the time and occasionally coughing blood I remembered Dr Richard Bell of Notting Hill. I had represented his young son on a serious charge of which he had been acquitted by the very just and sympathetic Magistrate, David Wacher. The young boy, aged about 18, had taken a lot of his father's drugs when the latter had gone off on his honeymoon with his second wife, a Vietnamese girl. Our defence was that the boy was so upset by being temporarily abandoned by his father that he did not realize what he was doing. This possibility was accepted by Mr Wacher, and the boy was acquitted. Richard had said: "If you ever need my help, just ring me." Well, I did – and I did!

But Richard himself did not come to me. His patients were not immune to the prevalent attack of influenza and he had not the time, but a Dutch doctor friend was visiting him and Richard sent him over with a syringe and a massive dose of penicillin. This doctor kept returning with more of the drug and eventually got me in his car to Dr Bell's clinic where double pneumonia was diagnosed, and it was found that a substantial part of one of my lungs had been destroyed by the disease. But with the aid of Richard and his Dutch friend I was on the mend, and keen to get back to my work on the Bench as soon as possible. Against their good advice I returned to work after five weeks, which was far too early, and therefore my recovery was never quite complete.

In 1974, just at the time when Eileen, my sister, died in hospital, I succumbed to another less severe attack of the same disease, but this time I was Court-wise and remained at home much longer.

It was during the first attack of pneumonia that I was transferred to Balham Magistrates' Court. This was appropriate, for it was held in a doctor's house on Balham High Road. It was unique in that only one stipendiary Magistrate sat there, and the ever-present Court reporter enabled one to make policies. During my first week of actually working there I noticed a preponderance of attacks by motorists on others whose mode of driving had displeased them. On my fourth day there I sentenced two such attackers, both men of otherwise good character, to short terms of imprisonment, warning other like-minded aggressive drivers that they should stay in their cars or they might expect similar penalties.

After this had been widely reported in the local papers a couple of days later I had no more such cases in the four months that I sat there. The Press can be very useful and influential at times. In this instance they (and I) probably saved several people from black eyes and loosened teeth. I think that a motor vehicle is such a potentially lethal weapon that everyone ought to have to undergo a psychological test of his patience under stress before being given a licence to drive; and that those who do find it necessary to deliver summary justice in physical form to others whose driving offends them should be subject to long periods of disqualification. But that is not the law.

Balham was for me a place of pleasant recollection even if, due to my lasting indisposition, I did have to sit with a scarf around my neck in a room heated only by a gasfire. I have only two unhappy memories of that now non-existent Court.

One was of one of the clerks there, a young man who would always interfere. The clerk's role in Court is a very delicate one: he should be a good lawyer, and also a good diplomat. He usually knows more law than the Magistrate does (that is certainly true in my case) but he should correct the Magistrate discreetly, and know when to keep quiet. He should not say loudly to the public at large, as did Gus Mindham, the Sergeant-Major of Bow Street, (the last of the legally unqualified clerks, and a very able man) once when I was sitting there as a Deputy:

"I'm sure that's a very good idea, sir, and one which most people would applaud. It's only a pity that the Divisional Court doesn't agree with you."

This Clerk at Balham lacked Mindham's experience, and irritated me immensely, to such an extent that I sought once to silence him when passing a somewhat complicated sentence by saying to the defendant:

"I shall now tell you what will happen to you. The learned Clerk will explain to you why it cannot happen, and then the jailor will take you away, because it will happen!"

Believe it or believe it not, it all took place exactly as I had predicted with a long and – to me – incomprehensible explanation by the Clerk as to why my sentence (which was not appealed) was illegal. That Clerk is now engaged in academic law, a field in which I am sure that he is much happier.

The other sad memory of Balham is of a case of a young man who had been in a lot of quite serious trouble, but starting only when he was 20, quite a late age for the commencement of a criminal career in south-west London. As is so often the case with Cockney families, although not always with the more well-to-do, his parents were there, anxiously awaiting the outcome of the proceedings. Realizing this, I asked the father to come forward from the public gallery. "I notice," I remarked, "that your boy was never before the Juvenile Courts, that his first conviction was at the age of 20. What went wrong in his life at that time?"

The father bowed his head and spoke with quiet dignity: "That was when his younger brother was hanged for murder."

I looked again at the surname of the defendant in the Court Register; it was Bentley.

My first Court on appointment was South-Western, and I did not like it very much. This may have been due to a most unfortunate experience that took place within a few days of my arrival there. A police officer came to see me in my room, a practice that I have firmly discouraged ever since this incident. "I wonder if you'd mind just signing this warrant, sir" he said casually but persuasively. "We've been trying to get hold of this chap for a long time. We think we know where to locate him now."

I read the document. "But it's just for speeding," I commented, "and he was only doing 41 miles an hour."

"Yes, I know, sir," went on the officer suavely, "but he's been trying all this time to avoid service. He's obviously a totter." (Even I knew that this last expression meant that the officer was alleging that the defendant was due for mandatory disqualification – not that he was engaged in the scrap-metal business.)

"Well, if you say so," I weakened, for the officer had obviously been in the job longer than I had.

It was the following Saturday morning that John Smith – and that really was his name – landed in his car from a Channel crossing with his second wife, their honeymoon just completed. What that unfortunate lady thought as her newly-wed husband was seized by police officers and led off to the cells at Dover Police Station I shall probably never know.

By Monday morning he had been transferred – in custody – to London, and at about 11 o'clock he appeared before me trembling with a mixture of fear and rage. He had not appeared at Court before, he explained, because he did not know of the proceedings. Following his divorce from his first wife he had moved about a lot before travelling in Europe on his recent honeymoon. A company director, aged about 40, he produced a clean driving licence. He had spent two nights in custody for his first and only offence, driving at 41 m.p.h. – and on my warrant! I think – I hope – that I dealt with the case by means of an absolute discharge. I know that I delivered to Mr Smith an abject apology, at the end of which we appeared to part as good friends who had had a little misunderstanding.

But it was not so. A few days later there arrived the "personal" letter from Mr Smith's solicitors claiming damages from me for wrongful arrest, false imprisonment, negligence and one or two other torts. I tried to get hold of the police officer, but was told that he had gone on long leave. I approached the Chief Clerk, who was not very interested – he had still not forgiven me for my late arrival on my first day, a couple of weeks earlier (see *Last in the List*, p. 268) – so he delegated the duty of replying to two of his junior clerks. Fortunately David Davies and Donagh Gleeson were both good lawyers – I have been lucky in recent times to have both of them with me at Horseferry Road Court where David Davies was the Senior Chief Clerk and Donagh Gleeson, deserving in my view of higher office than he has attained, was his most able assistant, and between them they produced a reply so skilful and legalistic that I think Mr Smith must have felt glad that nothing worse had happened to him. At any rate, I heard nothing further from those solicitors and am eternally grateful to those two excellent clerks for their successful joint efforts on my behalf, for they seemed at the time to have saved me from a fate far worse than death, even if I do still have a bit of a bad conscience over the unfortunate Mr John Smith.

So I did not care much for South-Western, where I had this bad experience, and did not get on well with the Chief Clerk, who is reported to have said of me: "He thinks he's Lord Goddard!" – which, having appeared before that formidable Chief Justice, I regarded as a compliment. The building itself, the first of the Aarvold Courts, was (and is) an ugly glorified pre-fab. I was not sorry to be moved from there after about five weeks.

It was some four years or so later, when I was at Thames, that an official of the Lord Chancellor's Department whom I met on a social occasion, remarked:

"That was a cunning move of yours to try to get back to South-Western."

"I don't understand. What do your mean?"

"Well, South-Western is the easiest London Court for you to get to, isn't it, and Thames is the most difficult?"

"True. Tell me more."

"So you got Rudy Narayan, a personal friend of yours, to write to the Lord Chancellor to say that one of the present Magistrates at South-Western has a strong colour prejudice and should be moved out of an area with a large black population, and that you understand the West Indians and are respected by them and you should be moved in. We all saw through it in the Department, of course."

I was astounded. Rudy had never spoken or written to me about a matter so fundamentally to affect my future.

"Well, I knew nothing about it," I asserted. The man from the Lord Chancellor's Department smirked his disbelief. "I'm afraid you don't believe me," I complained. "So offer me the next appointment to South-Western when a vacancy occurs in the normal way, and see what happens."

Not long after this Dennis Smith – not the Magistrate of whom Rudy had complained – was appointed a Crown Court Judge, and I was offered his position, and I declined, staying on at Thames for another year or two.

I do think Rudy should have consulted me . . .

The system which used to obtain for the disposition of Metropolitan Stipendiary Magistrates was that shortly after appointment they would go to Bow Street for a year for training with the Chief Magistrate and the

Principal Chief Clerk, then to Wells Street for up to a year, then to the next Court to fall vacant through death or retirement that nobody else wanted; thereafter one would not be moved unless one applied for a change when a vacancy was notified, and such vacancies would normally be filled strictly according to the seniority of the applicants. The main exceptions to this were Bow Street and Marlborough Street which (save for the new boy going to Bow Street) were, by tradition, always in the gift of the Lord Chancellor. (But all this has been changed by the present Chief Magistrate, Sir David Hopkin.)

Well, I had only three weeks at Bow Street. I have never been sure whether this was because I was so good that I needed only three weeks of training or because I was so bad that it was realized that no amount of training would make me improve; in fact I think the sensible solution probably was that Sergeant-Major Mindham, the Chief Clerk, did not like me. Anyway, I was transferred quickly from Bow Street to Balham and early in 1969 was notified of my move to Wells Street.

I hated it there. I do not like trying traffic cases, which are messy at the best of times, because people do not carry their driving licences or bring them to Court (or have them at all) and nowadays the computer at Swansea often does not produce the print-out in time (or at all).

Once when I got really fed up with the repeated failure of the Director of the Vehicle Licensing Centre in Swansea to produce the requisite print-out relating to a defendant, I asked my clerk, Roland Rees, to write an indignant letter to the Department saying that the Magistrate was thinking of issuing a witness summons against the Director personally. This did evince a reply. A computerized letter arrived saying that the Director regretted that he could not deal with the matter because Mr Roland Rees had omitted to supply his date of birth!

At Wells Street it was worse: most of the vehicles were stationary! One was dealing frequently just with parking offences – perhaps 150 in the morning, a similar number in the afternoon, twice a week. It was so boring . . . Often while I was there I would sit in my wretched little room in that horrid building and sigh to myself: did I really give up the excitement of life at the Bar for this? How Christopher Besley, the

Senior Stipe there when I arrived, stuck it for over 20 years I shall never know. For my part I was always on the phone to Sir Frank Milton, the Chief Magistrate asking: "When are you going to get me out of here?" until at last he silenced me by saying: "Methinks the lady doth protest too much", and my penance was a total of 15 months before I was transferred to Thames, geographically the most inaccessible Court from my home, a distance of 15 miles by car or attainable by public transport by using six different vehicles, a journey of nearly two hours in the rush-hour, either way. But once I got there, usually about 10.28 a.m., Thames was marvellous!

Wells Street was not, however. It had a Chief Clerk, Shaw, who had been there far too long and thought he had to make all the decisions. A vicious thug of a bus driver, represented by his Union, pleaded Not Guilty before me to an assault occasioning actual bodily harm on a taxi driver who he thought had "cut him up". The case had been transferred from a busier Court (Marylebone). He had leaped from his vehicle in Edgware Road, dragged the elderly and frail taxi-driver from his cab and felled him with one hard and well-aimed blow before strutting proudly back to drive off his crowded bus. The woman passenger in the taxi described it as the most horrifying experience of her life. I found the case proved and gave the bus driver a month. Shaw was quickly in Court. "You can't do that," he told me. "Why not?" I asked "The maximum is six months, isn't it?"

"We've got no cells here," said Shaw, "and I don't allow my Magistrates to send anyone to prison. You'll have to come back into Court and change it to a fine."

"I'm not going back," I said. "He deserves a month and he'll serve a month. The police will have to take him to prison." They did, and he did not appeal.

Soon after this Shaw came to see me and said: "You've got a hard day before you today. There are 221 in the morning list for companies failing to make annual returns. I want you to get through those in the morning because we've got the whole afternoon set aside for the case of a woman accused of running an unregistered school. There are lots of children to give evidence and it's set down for three hours, so I want there to be a prompt start at two." These requests could have been more delicately expressed, but they made good sense.

In fact I did not finish the Companies Act cases, with which I was wholly unfamiliar, before about 1.45, and in view of the obvious urgency of the other matter I decided to forgo lunch. Sitting in my room waiting to be called back into Court I discovered that running an unregistered school could not be all that serious an offence as it carried a maximum penalty of a fine of £20. I waited and waited and eventually called in the usher and the clerk. Everybody was there, I was told, except the prosecutor, another Mr Smith, a solicitor. I had met him once before, when I had defended his wife on a charge of careless driving. The case was a return brief of Robin Simpson, and the solicitor expressed himself very unhappy at my being substituted for the undoubtedly more experienced Robin. The result was good, I thought: an absolute discharge with no endorsement. But Smith did not think so. "Simpson would have got her off," he complained.

Where was Mr Smith, at 2.20 p.m.? Nobody knew. Had he telephoned the Court to say that he would be late? No, said the Clerk (not Shaw, but a junior clerk) adding slyly: "We know Mr Smith here. Perhaps he is having one of his long lunches." For good measure the Warrant Officer also present (they had no jailors at Wells Street) added: "I am afraid that our experience is that he is a gentleman who thinks that the Court is run for his personal convenience," "I'm coming into Court," I said, and I did. The advocate for the accused then got up and said: "I appear for the defendant and my friend Mr Smith appears for the prosecution – or rather he does not appear. I ask for the case to be dismissed." After further, more formal, inquiries about the whereabouts of Mr Smith, I acceded to his request. "And I ask for costs," persisted the defending advocate. I awarded these, in the sum of 10 guineas, and was advised by the Clerk that these had to be not against the Department of Education and Science but against the informant, who was – Mr Smith. I think this personal order for costs was to rankle considerably with the absent solicitor.

I went to my room. A few minutes later Gerda, my wonderful West Indian usher, knocked, and said: "Mr Smith has just arrived and he's demanding to see you."

"Does he want to apologize?" I enquired.

"I don't think so," she said quietly, "judging by the way he was speaking to me he's in a very belligerent mood."

"Then I shan't see him," I decided. "Tell him to go away." Having established that I could not help any of the other three Courts I went to the theatre and enjoyed a matinée; one of the only two free afternoons that I have had in working days in 21 years as a Magistrate.

Shortly afterwards an article about the case, headed "The Rush to Justice," appeared in the *New Law Journal*. It was written anonymously, but it would not need much imagination to identify the writer. The case, it was said, was a Marylebone case, which had been transferred to Wells Street (a mile and a half away) and the prosecuting solicitor had gone to Marylebone Court, realized his mistake, and hurried to Wells Street, only to find this important case dismissed by, it was implied, an impatient Magistrate, who cared little for justice. "Not even 10 minutes, but only five minutes after the case had been due to begin," the writer complained, "the prosecuting solicitor arrived, only to find that the summons had already been dismissed in his absence. The error on the prosecuting solicitor's part does not explain, and certainly does not excuse, the wholly unreasonable reaction of Mr Raymond (sic) Crowther, the Wells Street Magistrate, who was told that the prosecuting solicitor was on his way." (This was completely untrue.) "When the prosecuting solicitor arrived, a mere five minutes late, to find all was over the Magistrate had already left the building." (In fact, due to having to look through and sign some papers, I left just after three.)

If I suspect that the author of this article was Mr Smith, some support of that view may be found in an interview which that solicitor gave to the *Daily Telegraph*, in which he said that he had arrived only five minutes late and added: "This is the first time I have ever come across a Court behave (sic) in this way in 14 years' practice." The Department of Education and Science made a formal complaint about me to the Lord

Chancellor. It contained nothing untrue and was not upheld.

Now, 20 years later, with many more complaints under my belt (some justified, some not) I wonder why I worried so much about this trivial little case carrying a maximum penalty of £20 in which I ordered the complainant solicitor to pay costs of 10 guineas – but I did worry about it! It quite spoiled what otherwise would have been an idyllic holiday in his home in Southern Ireland which Kenneth Richardson (now an Old Bailey Judge) lent to us. Soon after the articles in the *Telegraph* (not, as might be imagined, the greatest supporter of the Judiciary) and the *Law Guardian* I received a telephone call from Anthony Babington, then a Stipendiary Magistrate at Marylebone and afterwards a Crown Court Judge at Knightsbridge. He told me that he was unable to understand how Smith had made a mistake as to the venue of the trial as when he had applied for the summons he had asked that the hearing should be held at Wells Street as he said that Marylebone was always too busy to devote a whole afternoon to such a case . . .

Not long afterwards I found myself at a cocktail party. A fellow guest asked me my occupation and I replied cautiously, as I usually do on such occasions: "I'm a lawyer."

My companion rose to the occasion. "What do you think," he demanded, "of that awful Magistrate who wouldn't wait even five minutes for a solicitor although he was told he was on his way? Do you know that at half-past two the Magistrate was on the golf course?"

"I think you should be careful," I replied. "I happen to know that the Magistrate has only played golf once in his life and detests the game."

"Well, my friend saw him there," he replied, determinedly.

"I think you should be extremely cautious before you repeat that story any more," I said. "I happen to know that the Magistrate went to the theatre that afternoon. I am the Magistrate concerned."

At that point my informant moved quietly away to another group at the party.

Chapter 3

The Drunks

Thames is (or was) a special Court. Since I wrote this it has been replaced by a large modern edifice, but in its old form it was just what a Magistrates' Court should be, ensconced in the area of the people it served so that they did not have to make an extensive and expensive journey to get justice. (I am not a believer in the modern concept of the large "Aarvold Courts".)

When I went there in 1970 Thames was in the heart of London's East End. It was still an area of damaged buildings showing the searing scars of the heaviest and most persistent bombing suffered by any part of Britain in World War II. These derelict buildings ("the derries", as the occupants called them) provided nocturnal shelter for many of those who suffered from one of the country's most chronic diseases: alcoholism.

There were over 120 cases in the list on the first morning that I arrived; a bit of a shock after the leisurely life of Wells Street. "Don't worry," said the jailor cheerfully, as he saw me gaping at the list. "Over a hundred of those are the usual drunks or d and ds" (drunk and disorderly cases). "The Colonel (Colonel Batt) and Mr Campion used to have a race to see who would get through them more quickly. They both got it down to under an hour. See if you can improve on that, sir." I had no intention of "improving on that" in the sense in which the jailor intended it.

The technique of these two impatient predecessors of mine had produced the following pattern:

Clerk: "Were you drunk?"

Defendant: "Yes."

Clerk: "Anything to say?"

Defendant: "Sorry."

Magistrate: "What's known?"
Jailor: "Many previous, sir. Here yesterday, when your colleague fined him £2 or one day."
Magistrate: "Very well, £3."
Defendant: "Time to pay, sir?"
Magistrate: "Or one day."

The jailor then immediately released the defendant, in readiness for opening time.

To the daily group of on-lookers in the public gallery the drunks at Thames were figures of fun, just as the prostitutes at Bow Street and Marlborough Street constituted the daily fashion parade of glamour girls. (It was always 40 shillings or one day for them at that time. Now the maximum sentence for soliciting for an immoral purpose is a fine of £400.) But should these little dramas be put on at all? Would it not be better to leave Harry Hall and John Dooley and Daniel Crampsey and Paddy Nolan and hundreds like them, who seem to do no harm to anyone, to die in their alcoholic stupors, rather than having them interfered with by police and jailors and clerks of Courts and Magistrates? But is it interfering or caring? It is often quite difficult to draw the line between the two. The Pharisee who left the man attacked by thieves to die in the gutter could certainly not be accused of interference. The same situation sometimes arises in New York and in London today. Sometimes an intention not to interfere is only another way of expressing indifference. Yet few of us would like to be what the law calls the "officious by-stander".

Sally Trench was a teenager when she missed her last train home to Surrey and found herself stranded at Waterloo for the night. She saw the meths drinkers huddled in their overcoats on the seats of the station, all their worldly possessions in carrier bags at their feet, being moved on every two hours or so by officers of the British Transport Police, asking, incredibly, if they were bona fide travellers. She felt such compassion for them that she sneaked out of her warm country abode each night and cycled up to Waterloo with coffee and sandwiches and cigarettes. Eventually they took her to their hearts and invited her to their real homes, the bomb sites of the Cut and Stepney, where she shared in the ritual of passing round the bottle in this twilight world. For years she lived with them and several of them died with her. "Bury me with my boots, Sal," were the last words of one, who had given his life heroically for a younger man when both were trapped by fire in a "derry", and this tribute to footwear, the tramp's most valued possession, was to provide Sally with the title of her world-famous book. She cared, but should the Courts? And should the public, whom the Courts are supposed to represent? I think they should.

There is another aspect to this problem. In certain regions there are few parks and open spaces, and post-war planners made the mistake of herding families into multi-storey flats without adequate playgrounds for children or recreation spaces for teenagers and adults. If such open spaces as there are are occupied, as they tend to be, by prematurely old men and women, living from hand to mouth (a bottle in the hand on the way to the mouth), this can expose young mothers to very real and justifiable fears for the safety of their children, causing them to shun those open spaces and lock themselves up on the fourteenth floors of their tower-like homes, because they realize that people affected by drink can behave in a way which is frightening and dangerous.

They are quick to quarrel and to fight, they expose themselves and urinate in public when they lack the time and energy to reach the places which a thoughtful public corporation provides for that purpose, and they rob and steal when they see no other way of obtaining the answer to their greatest and only desire – their next drink; and sometimes they molest small children. So the law must show some care and exercise some control if public parks are not to become private hovels.

It was for these reasons that I refused to go along with the "£3 or one day" routine so popular with most of the jailors, and started remanding the drunks for medical reports and social inquiry reports. I had not been doing this for long whan a knock came at the door of my room one lunchtime. It was the "Duty" Probation Officer. Unlike every other probation officer that I have met – for the vast majority are really good, dedicated people – he was unpleasant, brusque and politically motivated. "Look here," he said angrily, "the staff have got quite enough to do without all these extra remands for reports for the drunks. They're dirty, smelly and not worth wasting time on. If you carry on like this, you'll have a strike on your hands."

It so happened that just at that time a friend gave me a copy of *Bury Me with My Boots*, which I found a most moving chronicle. I wrote to Sally Trench and explained my problem and she came to Thames Court to see for herself. Some of the defendants she recognized. A week later Sally came again with two prominent members of Alcoholics Anonymous, and over lunch in my room we drew up a plan of campaign. Every day there would be in Court a member of A.A. and he would signal to me the one or two drunks of the morning who seemed to have reached rock-bottom and therefore to be receptive of immediate help – for the Duty Probation Officer was right in suggesting that you cannot help all the alcoholics all the time – and I would introduce such defendants to the A.A. representative who would take them to A.A. meetings and personally care for them.

This scheme had been in operation for only a couple of days when an even louder knock came at my door. "Look here, Mr Crowther, you've gone too far this time. You've called in outside people to do probation officers' work. The Union won't stand for it. Either those men come out of your Court tomorrow or you'll have no probation officers working for you next week." For once I lost my customary cool. "You're a dog in the manger," I adjudged. "You won't do the work yourself and you won't let anyone else do it. I'm not going to be told how to run my Court by you."

He calmed down at that, and we worked out a compromise. The A.A. man would signify to me those he believed would be responsive to help but then I should hand them over to the Probation Service who would prepare reports. The Senior stipulated that there should be never more than three such referrals a day, but the A.A. experts thought this was unlikely, anyway.

This scheme operated reasonably successfully during the three and a half years I spent at Thames and I like to think that it saved a few sunken souls from a wretched life and an undignified death, although I understand from my current colleagues at Thames that Harry Hall still appears regularly in the dock, 20 years on; and one regular at West London whom I tried to help expired one night of swallowing his own alcoholic vomit on the steps of West London Court to which he had crept back to die, like a wounded animal trying to get to its lair.

Sally Trench was an idealist and a worker, and when she suspected that somebody else might be an idealist she determined to make that person work for her. So it came about that soon after I was chairman of "Project Spark", a scheme under which Sally bought up a terrace of derelict houses in a run-down part of Leeds and installed in them jobless boys just leaving Borstal whose task was to renovate the houses; after which these would be let to homeless families, their rents paid or subsidized by the local authority, and the boys would move on to the restoration of other derelict properties. Sally provided me with a strong committee, including the Hon. David Astor who was such a sweet, kind man that it was difficult to believe that he was a newspaper proprietor.

Project Spark was not a great success because – predictably – the boys did not work very hard and – understandably – they did not want to move out of the original houses once they had made them reasonably comfortable.

And I was also to become involved in Alcoholics Anonymous. I received an invitation to lunch from the National Chairman, Ronald R. (All members of A.A. are called by their Christian names and the initial of their surnames; this is their guarantee of anonymity.) "You choose the wine," he said graciously, as wc sat down in the sumptuous restaurant on the top floor of St. George's Hotel, just by Broadcasting House and opposite the British Council Student Centre. So opulent did everything seem that I chose a Gévrey-Chambertin.

"No, only one glass," Ronald ordered the waiter.

"I am sorry, how could I have been so stupid?" I apologized. "Of course I won't have any wine."

"No, you have it, if you enjoy it," said Ronald generously. "It has no effect on me now to see others drinking. But I hope if, five years ago, before I joined A.A. you had seen me lying in the gutter, as I did nearly every night, you would not have been one of those who kicked me as you went past." "I don't think so," I murmured, and Ronald went on to tell me that he had been a prominent surveyor before a tragedy in his personal life had produced the greater tragedy of excessive drinking. At last someone had introduced him to A.A., and now he was the surveyor to all the Queen's estates, a post that he obviously merited, for he was one of the most intelligent and articulate men I have ever met. Tragically he died young a couple of years later of a sudden heart attack, to be succeeded by the ebullient Gordon B.

At the end of the meeting, and the bottle of Gévrey-Chambertin, I was on the Committee of Alcoholics Anonymous, a "non-alcoholic member", which meant that I was allowed to drink alcohol and to use my full name. My main task was to introduce defendants with a drinking problem to the organization, and this I followed with enthusiasm thereafter. It is a fact that if prohibition were successfully introduced and in addition all sales of illegal drugs could be stopped many Magistrates could be made redundant, for the vast majority of crimes other than motoring offences are drink and drug related.

I remained with A.A. for many years, attending four day-long meetings in London each year and one annual week-end conference in Manchester, and I have seldom come across a more admirable body of men and women. It is the only organization of which I have been a member which is completely class-unconscious, for its members recognize that drink is no respecter of persons and attacks people in all walks of society.

Oddly enough, my reason for resigning from A.A. was due to another addiction, smoking. I had my last cigarette on my thirtieth birthday, resolving never to smoke again, and I hate the habit.

It is my misfortune that all members of my family smoke heavily, but I can hardly resign from my family. But when I went to those A.A. meetings everybody except me smoked and chain-smoked and the atmosphere after eight hours of this behind the closed windows of an hotel in Earls Court resembled the worst days of the London smog; about 30 of them would get through a total of nearly 1,500 cigarettes in the day and I would return exhilarated by the dedicated discussion, but depressed by a severe headache resulting from the narcotic poison. The Committee members had simply substituted one drug addiction for another.

In 1974 I had suffered my second attack of pneumonia, and my lungs are not complete, and various doctors have advised me of the danger of passive smoking so, rather selfishly, I resigned and, rather hypocritically, I gave pressure of work as the excuse. I could not bring myself to tell these good people of the true reason, but perhaps some of them will learn of it now.

The Chairman was anxious that a member of the Judiciary should remain on the Committee, and I proposed Judge Edward Clarke, Q.C., an ardent pipe-smoker, who accepted readily; he had not long to go as an Old Bailey Judge, so would have ample time in retirement for A.A. activities, and the body was pleased to have him. For my part it gave me the opportunity to restore my association with Edward after what he regarded as my disgraceful misconduct in the Cumberland Lodge affair, of which I have written elsewhere in this book, and I was glad to heal the breach.

Johnny was one who benefited from Alcoholics Anonymous – eventually. He came before me frequently at West London for drug offences – he was a heroin addict – and for being drunk, and drunk and disorderly, and for petty thefts designed to provide him with the means to support his addictions. (It costs at least £100 a day to sustain the habit of heroin, and this does not come out of one's social security.)

Johnny was not a man born with a silver spoon in his mouth. His mother was white and his father coloured. She left his father soon after Johnny was born because of the father's violence, and mother and son went to live in a Salvation Army Hostel, where the mother abandoned Johnny two years later. It was little wonder, perhaps, that he started getting into trouble at the age of nine.

Johnny reminds me of our first encounter outside the Court setting when I met him in Hammersmith Road by chance and said "I wish you could give up the drink and the drugs. I'm sure you're a decent man really and could lead a happy and a useful life," and I gave him one of the Alcoholics Anonymous cards that I always had with me in Court.

Johnny was fairly drunk at the time, and did not immediately make use of the card, but he was able to remember the incident because "it was the first time anyone in authority had spoken gently to me." But the thefts went on and eventually the time came when it was necessary to remove Johnny from the drug scene and his alcoholic associates and I gave him three months.

He celebrated his release eight weeks later by getting drunk and disorderly again. But the period in prison had improved his health and solid food had enabled him to gain some weight. I said "It's a pity if you return to the drink after a couple of months off it. I'll have some more reports about you and grant you bail on condition that you reside at a dry-house in the East End and do not visit any public house or off-licence." (Such bail conditions would be illegal now!) Johnny adhered to the conditions and looked fit when he reappeared a month later. Then I deferred sentence for three months, and it was then that he took the card out of his jacket pocket and started attending A.A. meetings.

It was over a year before I heard from Johnny again. Then I received a letter from him at my Court. In it he said that he wanted to thank me for the three-month sentence and for the period in the dry-house, that he had been alcohol-free and drug-free ever since, was feeling fitter than he ever remembered being, had just got his own council flat and was working as a painter and decorator. He went on to say that he wanted to thank me personally, and to discuss a project that he hoped to set up. It all sounded so genuine that I invited him to lunch at the little Italian restaurant that I used to frequent around the corner from West London Court, first advising Maria (the proprietress) that – exceptionally – under no circumstances was alcohol to be presented.

Johnny told me that he had become convinced that drugs were an even greater problem than alcohol among young people, especially in the area of Kensington and Earls Court. Alcoholics Anonymous had originated in America where now there was a flourishing sister organisation called Narcotics Anonymous. Johnny had the opportunity of setting up a branch of N.A. with meetings in St. Mary Abbott's Hospital in Kensington. Would he have my support? The answer was emphatically "Yes", and I have attended many N.A. meetings organized by Johnny all over West London, and due to his efforts the organization has successfully spread throughout the country.

Johnny rings me about once a month to give me a progress report on N.A. and it is always cheerful, optimistic and encouraging. On New Year's Eve 1989 he rang me just to wish me a happy New Year. Once though, he phoned in a state of great depression. He had been invited to address N.A. meetings in the United States but had been refused a visa because of his previous record of "moral turpitude". I was able, arguing from the terms of the Rehabilitation of Offenders Act 1972, to persuade the U.S. Consul-General to reverse this decision. I said that I felt that I could guarantee that Johnny would do no harm but only good in the United States, and Johnny got his visa.

He was such a success that he was asked to return next year, when there were similar visa difficulties, but these were overcome this time by a single telephone call, since when Johnny has been lecturing in many other countries including Germany and Ireland, and he never forgets to send me a cheery card to supplement his monthly telephone calls. He is now specializing in helping Italian drug addicts in this country who are H.I.V. positive and is planning to attend a drugs conference in Italy later this year.

I think that I admire Johnny more than anyone else I have seen in Court – certainly more than anyone else in the dock; a former alcoholic and drug addict, he surely did not fall into the category of someone "not worth wasting time on", to use the words of my former Duty Probation Officer. Johnny has certainly saved many, many young lives and deserves to be condemned only by the drug dealers for his desertion of them.

But more needs to be done on an official basis. It should not be left to voluntary organizations like A.A. and the Salvation Army (affectionately known as the "Sally Ally") to save something from the wrecks of these wretched, wasted lives.

Many years ago the local authority in Leeds set up a Detoxification

Centre which proved highly successful. (It has recently had to close when public funds were withdrawn from it; "the drunks" are not a very productive part of our society.) I felt that such a centre was needed in London's East End and so I inquired into the possibilities. A dedicated doctor called Denham (sorry, that sounds rather like the start of a limerick!) showed great interest and offered me premises which I went to see in the Gordon Hospital, a part of the London Hospital Group.

All that we needed now was money to pay the staff. The Secretary of State for Social Services at that time was Sir Keith Joseph. I put to him my project. The drunks, who at that time were frequently being sentenced to up to 30 days imprisonment when my colleague and I felt this necessary to save their lives, should be given the option of a period in the Detoxification Centre, where they would receive medical attention and visits from members of A.A., who would meet them on their release. If they were able to remain "dry" for a long period following departure from the Detoxification Centre they would be encouraged to find work (many had been good workers until they lost their sobriety) and would be aided finally, after perhaps a year without alcohol, to achieve the ultimate in self-respect for which inwardly most of these people really long, a little flat of their own.

It has always been my policy when I have had what I thought was a good idea to go right to the top. That was why I wrote to Keith Joseph. I was most encouraged by his response and his interest. He wanted precise details of how the scheme would work. I was able to supply them. We corresponded for many months. The Secretary of State surprised me greatly by the caring compassion that he displayed for a group of people who would not normally go to the polls. I have written to many Ministers in my time. Keith Joseph was the only one, apart from Cecil Parkinson, who replied to all my letters personally, in long hand, and within days of receiving them. In the result he agreed to the provision of a million pounds a year for my project, and Dr Denham was eagerly awaiting the first cheque for his work.

Then came the miners' strike of 1974 and Edward Heath called a general election, asking the people to support him against that then mighty union, the N.U.M. They did not do so. Barbara Castle replaced Keith Joseph as Secretary of State for Social Services. Dr Denham waited in vain for his cheque. I wrote many personal letters to Mrs Castle, which for a long time were ignored. Eventually I got a typed reply from an official purporting to write on her behalf saying that the Secretary of State had given due consideration to my project, but the new Labour Government had other much more important schemes commanding far higher priorities. The Detoxification Centre was never set up. "Those people", the drunks, were consigned once more to the bottom of the human dustbin.

Sir Keith Joseph, an austere, ascetic man, but a brilliant speaker, following a period as Secretary of State for Education, has been declared *persona non grata* by many student unions. If he comes to speak to them the students are not prepared to listen, but will have eggs and tomatoes ready for him. Well, he was prepared to listen to me and my supplications on behalf of a most unfortunate and impoverished section of society.

But there has been a great change of attitude on the part of the Probation Service since I went to Thames 20 years ago. All the Seniors I know recognize alcohol (as well as drugs) as being a most potent factor in the rising crime statistics and are determined to combat it with sympathy and understanding. This is especially true of my last Court, Horseferry Road, where one probation officer, John Smith, has become a specialist in dealing with "these people" and, treating them in a humane and realistic manner, has had some staggering successes. We have come a long way since that Probation Officer at Thames, and the "£3 or one day" routine of Cecil Campion and the Colonel.

But Thames was indeed a special Court. On my first day there was a knock on my door and a large man with dark horn-rimmed spectacles entered and addressed me in a strong Cockney accent: "Good morning, Mr Crowther. I'm Charlie, Charlie Patterson. Now, I've got a question for you. Are you a hard-liner or a do-gooder?" "I'd like to think I am somewhere between the two," I replied somewhat apprehensively, believing that I was in the presence of some powerful official from the

Home Office. (In fact Charlie was a fairly lowly clerk at Thames.)

"No, that won't do at all, Mr Crowther," he retorted severely. "We don't want any of that wishy-washy stuff. We thought bloody old Springer was going to be tough when he came here" – he was referring to my highly respected senior colleague – "but he's gone all soft on us. Why, the other day I even caught him talking to the duty Probation Officer!" (His aversion to this particular individual I was to come to understand.) "Now listen. I've been burgled four times and it's driving my wife crazy, but all the bloody J.P.s do is give them a small fine which they never pay and a pat on the bo-bo." "I'll bear in mind what you say Mr Patterson, but each case must be decided on its merits." Mr Patterson withdrew, looking disappointed in me. He had made one of the very few efforts to influence my decision-making and had not succeeded.

I am often asked if the Government does not try directly to influence my decisions and those of other Magistrates and Judges. The answer, so far as I am concerned, is emphatically "No". The independence of the Judiciary is profoundly respected.

But despite what I regarded as a highly improper initial approach I came to like and admire Charlie. A conscientious worker with his heart in the right place, there was a rôle for him in the administration of Justice. His repeated applications to become a Justice of the Peace were inevitably rejected, no doubt because he expressed to the interviewing committee the same sort of opinions that he had voiced to me on my first day at Thames.

Yet his point of view is undoubtedly shared by a significant proportion of the British public and, if the lay judiciary is to be truly representative, should there not have been a place for Charlie on the lay bench, where he could always be outvoted if his approach were too extreme? I tend to think that when dealing with serious crime lay benches nowadays are too soft and are not adequately protecting the public.

Recently a lay justice from Suffolk sat with me for a day as an observer. Of 50 defendants appearing before me that morning three had finished up with immediate prison sentences. She was appalled. "I've been sitting as a justice for nearly a year now," she protested, "and no

Bench of which I have been a member has ever sent anyone to immediate imprisonment."

"Not even when they have already been subject to suspended sentences?" I inquired.

"No, the Home Secretary is always urging us to avoid sending people to prison. Don't you know that the prisons are overcrowded?"

The influence of the politicians on decision-making is indirect rather than direct, covert rather than overt, and subject, like far too many things in our society, to considerations of immediate cost rather than far-sighted policy.

Charlie's considerable energy was expended once a year in the annual Thames Dinner-Dance, held at the swimming baths of the York Hall, Bethnal Green, which all stipendiaries, past and present, were expected to attend with their wives, on pain of lasting ignominy. It was a tremendous event at which one met socially persons whom one had seen in Court in all sorts of capacities. When Charlie eventually retired a couple of years ago it was I who had the privilege of making the presentation speech to this great Court character.

But a far more formidable figure at Thames than Charlie was the Court Matron, Mrs Brown, who had been there since time immemorial. I had been there a few weeks when Mrs Brown dropped in specially to see me.

"Mr Crowther, you've been accepted," she pronounced. "Oh good," I remarked nervously, "but for what?" "You don't understand," she replied severely. "You're accepted. The people here like you. They respect your judgments. They've told me so. It's important in a village like Thames." This last statement was true. I felt that I had really arrived when, a few days later, an unrepresented defendant said to me: "I know this is the sort of offence you don't like, Mr Crowther, but there are factors in mitiggeration."

It is much easier to influence the habits of local people in a small Court like the old Thames than in a big one like Horseferry Road (or the new Thames). And Mrs Brown was indeed a power in the Thames land. Indeed there were those who said that her influence continued after her death, which occurred not long after I came to Thames.

Her successor, Mrs Gumble, a much less flamboyant personality (but no less a strong one) swore that the ghost of Mrs Brown pervaded the Court long after the former matron had departed this life, that Mrs Brown was envious of Mrs Gumble and had put the "evil eye" upon her, and indeed two of my successors complained of the activities of Mrs Brown acting as a poltergeist throwing articles of furniture around in their room when apparently she disapproved of their decisions. I never had this experience; but then, I was accepted by Mrs Brown.

Mrs Gumble was not the type to try to influence the Court's decisions; yet she did once, and to good effect. A young woman of previous good character appeared before me, unrepresented, charged with a serious theft from her employer, an offence which, because of the element of breach of trust inherent in such a crime, in those days almost always carried an immediate sentence of imprisonment, which I was about to pass.

The Matron is always present in Court when a female prisoner is sentenced and on this occasion, to my surprise, Mrs Gumble intervened.

"May I speak, sir? I know this woman and her family very well. She is a good woman but unfortunately she's suffering from cancer. She had one breast removed a few weeks ago and she's got to go into hospital to have the other removed very soon. She's seriously ill, but she couldn't get the operations done quickly on the National Health because of the industrial action and she stole the money because she was desperate."

So I remanded the case for four weeks for a social inquiry report and the defendant finished up on probation. Next time the employer came along to say that he had forgiven the woman and did not want me to award compensation. In the meantime Mrs Gumble had got at him too.

At my next Court (West London) my Chief Clerk was to be the very severe, very learned, very remarkable Pat Austin. A friend who had tried to telephone me around 10 o'clock, reported back to me that Pat had regaled him with this message: "Ho! ho! ho! If you want to speak to Mr Crowther I suggest you ring between 10.28 and 10.30, because that's the only time that I ever see him except when he's in Court."

It is true that I do not arrive early (I like my sleep) although in 21 years I was only twice late (once when there was a burst water-main). But my habit of arriving only a minute or two before the Court sat did, I fear, cause many grey hairs in successive Chief Clerks who wondered if the Court would be able to start on time. It was therefore perhaps not without significance that when I left Thames for West London after three and a half happy years the gift that the Thames staff gave me, an inveterate voyager, was – a travelling alarm clock!.

Chapter 4

"The Battle for Cumberland Lodge"

"For evil to triumph requires only that good men do nothing." This well-known dictum of Edmund Burke hangs in my study, for I consider that, after the teachings of Christ, it is, in its implication of what is required of us, one of the most important doctrinal axioms that I have come across.

Amy Buller was an idealist, and one of those really formidable women that only this country seems capable of producing. But the formative years of her education took place in the 1930s in Germany, a country whose people she loved and admired. The greater therefore was her horror at the rise of Nazism, and her dismay at the absorption of some of her young German friends into that evil movement. She developed a theory that the failure of German intellectuals to nip Nazism in the bud, and, indeed, its attraction for many of them, lay in the singlemindedness with which German students specialized in their chosen subjects; that this led to blinkered vision and an unreadiness or a selfish unwillingness to perceive anything beyond their own ultimate goals.

She went on to say that such extremism and intolerance could equally well occur in Britain – and I agree with her, having seen some members of the National Front and the Socialist Workers' Party, who have much in common, in Court before me – and that the way to avoid it was by a cross-fertilization of the various disciplines, in order that every intellectual could get to know the other person's point of view, and that for this purpose a college was needed where students of all subjects could meet together in a relaxed atmosphere to discuss national and international problems.

To this end she wrote and published a book entitled *Darkness over*

Germany and, shortly after the war, this book came to be read by Her Majesty Queen Elizabeth, the mother of our present Queen, who was so fascinated by it that Amy Buller found herself invited to lunch by their Majesties at Royal Lodge in Windsor Great Park, where, during the afternoon, she expanded on her principles, saying that all she needed was a suitable building to put them into practice.

Cumberland Lodge is only about half a mile away from Royal Lodge. It had been given to the Duke of Cumberland (nicknamed "Butcher Cumberland") as a reward for the thoroughness, not to say the brutality, with which he had slaughtered a rebellious Scottish Army at Culloden Field, and it had remained in the hands of similar "noble" families as a Grace and Favour house until the end of the Second World War. But then, with a new spirit of independence pervading the whole British race, the acquisition of servants became extremely difficult and, not long after the end of World War II, Cumberland Lodge found itself vacant and abandoned. It was then that, according to Amy Buller, Queen Elizabeth said to the King over breakfast: "We can give Cumberland Lodge to Amy Buller for her college" and their Majesties lent their name to the Trust, calling it the "King George VI and Queen Elizabeth Foundation of St. Catherine's". Soon after that, Amy Buller's dream came true.

I was privileged to have a long conversation with her during which she explained to me her ideas, and my description of her as a formidable idealist is fully justified. But it was Lord Denning who got me involved in Cumberland Lodge. As a Bencher, and subsequently Treasurer, of Lincoln's Inn, he had the interests of law students, especially those from the Commonwealth, closer to his heart than any other prominent lawyer that I have ever known, and by the early 1960s he had organized that Bar students (many from Commonwealth countries) of Lincoln's Inn should have the opportunity, two or three times a year, of getting away from their law books to the spacious beauty of Windsor Park for a long weekend, during which they would meet informally the more senior members of the profession, the barristers and the Benchers including, always, the one they loved and admired most, Lord Denning himself. He called these week-ends, which were soon to be emulated by all the other three Inns, "The Law at Home", and no title could have been more appropriate.

By 1955, although only of four years' Call, I was conducting a weekly class in Advocacy for the Council of Legal Education – almost unbelievably the first such class that the Council had ever organized since its inception. Until quite recently a deaf mute could have been Called to the Bar and would have been qualified to conduct a case for a hapless client!

Lord Denning got to know of my classes and, my being a member of Lincoln's Inn, invited me down to devise and conduct some exercises in Advocacy during a week-end at Cumberland Lodge in the mid-fifties. With his help and encouragement (Lord Denning himself sometimes sitting as the smiling, kindly Judge) the session was a success and I think that I attended every such Lincoln's Inn Cumberland Lodge week-end (and also some such week-ends for the Inner and Middle Temples) until 1982 . . .

The atmosphere of "The Law at Home" engendered by Lord Denning was such that even the most fearsome and most erudite of the Chancery Judges, like Harman and Russell, emerged as warm human beings (I never remember seeing Roxburgh there). While still a relatively young barrister I entered the bar at Cumberland Lodge one evening and Lord Justice Russell, before whom I had appeared only once, and whom I found utterly terrifying but extremely entertaining, said gruffly: "Crowther, let me buy you a drink". I had a whiskey while he consumed what appeared to be a long drink from a half-pint tumbler. When we had both finished our libations I offered: "May I get you the same again?"

"You wouldn't be able to afford it," he replied, surprisingly. I was slightly indignant. "Try me," I said, "life isn't all that bad at the Bar." "Very well, you asked for it," he threatened (which was literally true), "the same again, barman, for both of us" and George, the ever-friendly George Nolan – the only member of the staff of those days who is still there – gave me a single measure of whiskey and filled the Lord Justice's tumbler with the same beverage. Yet, two hours later, after dinner and a further visit to the bar – during which I kept my distance from him – Lord Justice Russell gave, without notes, the most lucid and delightfully witty account of life at the Bar (the other Bar) that can possibly be imagined.

There were several Principals during my years at Cumberland Lodge; all, until 1982, decent men dedicated to Amy Buller's ideals. One, Robert McCallum, was a bit of a barrister manqué and the best thing that I could do for him was to extend an invitation to dine in Hall at Lincoln's Inn, the atmosphere of which enchanted him. The Cumberland Lodge of those days was a tolerant place and I was allowed to bring down for those glorious week-ends my family comprising Elke, my wife, my two young children, Eileen, my sister, and our large Labrador dog who, needless to say, loved the change of scenery and of trees. So kind were the staff that on more than one occasion the Principal moved out of his own house so that all my brood could adjourn to that comfortable abode. My sister, a very religious person and a dedicated monarchist, loved these week-ends because they enabled her to worship in the Chapel Royal and greet and be greeted by members of the Royal Family: security was virtually unnecessary in those halcyon days.

Mr McCallum died in harness and a year later his place was taken by the Senior Tutor, Edward Bannister, a young member of the Chancery Bar, who became "Acting Principal", an office which he held for two years. Edward was in some ways a rather forbidding person, for he was (and is) highly intelligent with a very ready wit, and he seldom smiles. Straight, straight-faced and apparently straight-laced he could (and would) say the most outrageous things and get away with them. There used to be a Christmas house party for lonely overseas students – perhaps the most useful activity that took place at Cumberland Lodge – and for many years I was to help to run it.

Once, after dinner on the first evening, we all assembled in the Tapestry Room and Edward announced, very solemnly: "Now. We're all going to have a game. All the girls go to the middle of the room and all the men stand in a circle around them. Right. Now, all the girls take your clothes off, except for those of you with big black bottoms."

Racist! Sexist! people nowadays would cry, but I watched the students' reactions and all the African women just laughed and laughed. Edward had judged well just how quickly they would have lost their inhibitions in the friendly, trusting atmosphere that was Cumberland Lodge.

But it was before that Christmas Party that I first got to know Edward Bannister well. Luvi, my Labrador, was thirsty, and after dinner I was taking him on a mile-long walk to the pub when we overtook Edward, who was on the same mission.

"I should like to extend our activities within Amy Buller's remit. Cumberland Lodge should not be a resort for rich people" (it was to become that, in 1982). "And I would like to attract a group that is under-privileged, yet cultured. Do you know of such a group?" "Yes," I replied, after a little thought. "Assistant teachers"; and I explained to Edward that they were young people who came over to England under the auspices of the Central Bureau (a Government organization) to teach their own languages (French, German, Spanish, and Italian) in our schools, being paid disgracefully low wages by the local authorities and often being shunned by the "real teachers", some of the more politically motivated of whom – and there were plenty of these in the 1960s and 70s – saw them as a source of cheap labour and "blacklegs", to be treated with contempt.

The Central Bureau gave one "Welcome" Party for them in the British Council Student Centre (until it closed in 1981) and then left them to their own devices. I think they were – and still are – shamefully treated.

"Good," commented Edward, "they sound exactly the sort of people we should be targeting. Will you organize a week-end for them?" It was to be the first of many, which hundreds of these young people will remember all their lives, and these "Assistant Teacher" week-ends, entitled "English Life and Language" continued until 1982.

I was invited to extend my activities, and started taking students from language schools, including my own, to Cumberland Lodge for week-ends. Usually my family accompanied me, to such an extent that we used presumptuously (but privately) to refer to this Royal Grace and Favour house as our "country home".

Edward became a good friend and even influenced me to share his passion for horse-riding, a pursuit that I shared with him until late 1974 when "my" horse, a most friendly animal, was not available and I was accorded another one. This creature regarded my not inconsiderable bulk with apprehension and then looked greedily for a lump of sugar, which I had forgotten that day, so he determined to teach me a lesson.

By now I was a fairly experienced horse-rider, allowed to gallop. This spiteful equine animal repeatedly got going at great speed and then stopped suddenly in his efforts to throw me off. He did not succeed, but he did put the fear of Pegasus into me to such an extent that when after an hour of this horror I eventually dismounted I was in cold sweat. Windsor is a long way from London and, by the time that I got back home on that cold and windy day, a fever was building up in me and soon I was confined to bed, for the second time in my life, with pneumonia, and I was not to ride again. If I had known as much then as I was to learn later I would have Christened this disagreeable quadruped "Lord Vaizey".

Edward Bannister began to build up a really good practice at the Chancery Bar and the work at Cumberland Lodge was getting too much for him, and in 1974 he indicated that he did not wish to continue as Acting Principal. By now I was organizing so many activities there that I felt that I knew more about the Lodge than anyone except Edward and Ruth Norton, the wonderful and devoted secretary who I think remembered everybody who had stayed there during the quarter of a century or so that she had held that post. So I decided to apply to be the Principal of Cumberland Lodge. Usually in my 20 years and more as a stipendiary Magistrate I have had extremely kind and co-operative colleagues, especially in those days at West London Court, where my "partner" was Peter Badge, shortly to be succeeded by the equally delightful Jimmy Cook. My plan was that I should do my four days at Court from Monday to Thursday, when I should drive out to Windsor organizing the Cumberland Lodge week-end until early Monday morning, when I would return to West London. My colleague would work the end of the week: Wednesday to Saturday. I felt sure Cumberland Lodge could be run by a part-time Principal with the full-time assistance of the loyal and knowledgeable Ruth Norton.

So I applied for the post. But it was not to be. Sir Frank Milton, then Chief Metropolitan Magistrate, got to hear about it and, to use an extreme understatement, he indicated his disapproval. By seeking part-time employment at Cumberland Lodge, he argued, I was implying that the position of stipendiary Magistrate was also part-time, which was not the case, as the terms of our engagement stipulated that we were all on call six days a week and must live within 15 miles of our base Court, whereas Cumberland Lodge was about 20 miles from London. Sir Frank was a forthright character for whom I always had the greatest respect, and I withdrew my application, intending never to renew it.

The new Principal was Walter James, a New Zealand journalist, a kindly but forgetful man very much like my then Director at the British Council Student Centre. Walter remained as Principal for eight years, during which my activities there continued, and I think that under his friendly aegis the Lodge flourished. It certainly became more formal and more structured, with various committees meeting to discuss matters of policy. At the beginning of June 1977 I received, "out of the blue" (or rather, out of the House of Lords) a letter from Lord John Vaizey inviting me to join the Cumberland Lodge Academic Advisory Committee in place of Judge Edward Clarke who had expressed a wish to retire:

> "I know how much you already do for the Lodge, and how concerned you are with legal education . . . I feel therefore that it is particularly fitting that we should turn to an old friend of the Lodge to ask for his assistance. I do hope you will be able to say yes. John."

I did say Yes and I attended all future meetings of the Academic Advisory Committee up to and including that of May 22nd, 1982.

I did not know Lord Vaizey personally. I was aware that he had been made a Life Peer by Harold Wilson in that Prime Minister's controversial Honours List of 1976 which included Lady Falkender; that not long afterwards he changed party and became a Conservative peer; that he had written to *The Times* saying how all his former friends and colleagues in the Labour Party had now "sent him to Coventry", and this was his reward in a democratic society for being true to his principles; and that a Labour Member of Parliament had replied that Vaizey was right, and no one on that side of the House would speak to him again, because he was an East End boy who had been nourished and nurtured by the Labour Party and that not long after he had got what he wanted he had crossed to the other side, betraying all those who had helped him.

My sympathies at the time were with John Vaizey. They were to change to the Labour Member.

One of the precepts to which I usually adhere is that having committed oneself to doing something one should do it, even if a more attractive offer comes along. I can think of just three occasions in my life when I have abandoned this principle, and on two of these I was bitterly to regret my change of mind. This was one of them.

John Williams is a solicitor living and practising around Bromley. He is a Justice of the Peace and sits occasionally as a deputy stipendiary. He is extremely active in the training of lay justices in south-east London and had invited me to help him run a training week-end at a place called Foxbury between May 21st and 23rd, 1982 and I had agreed. I let him down and he has never asked me again, and I don't blame him.

It was about 10 days before Foxbury that I chanced to meet Lord Justice Lawton in the Temple. "Fiery Fred", as he was popularly designated, was the greatest criminal lawyer that I have ever known. I hope I shall not be misunderstood if I say that Fred Lawton has spent his life in crime. His father was, I believe, a prison governor. My first vision of Fred was of his challenging (figuratively) Ewen Montague to a duel at Middlesex Sessions, and of Fred's winning, the only counsel whom I observed to achieve this feat other than the unfortunate Sir Harold Cassel. After a period as a highly successful silk, Fred was appointed a High Court Judge, in which capacity I appeared before him many times.

He had allocated to him most of the really important criminal cases, and was the Judge designated to try the Richardson gang. Ultimately he became a very distinguished Lord Justice of Appeal. Fred Lawton, a strong Judge who combined humanity with a lot of common sense, knew more about crime than anyone I have ever come across. This was the man who stopped me in the Temple.

"Eric. I'm taking part the week-end after next in a seminar on police powers at Cumberland Lodge. The Deputy Commissioner will be there, and Paul Boateng, and I think your experience as a Metropolitan Magistrate would be useful. Will you join us?"

I did not tell him about Foxbury; Fred would not have approved of my letting anybody down. But next day I 'phoned John Williams asking him to get someone in my place.

In some ways "Police Powers" was to be a scintillating week-end. Fred was brilliant, as ever, as he attacked "the so-called academics of the University of East Anglia who tell us how to do our job"; and the Deputy Commissioner highlighted the tightrope walked constantly by the police, with the axiom: "Too much control is tyranny; too much freedom is anarchy".

The surprise to me was Paul Boateng. He was (or was to become) the Greater London Council's spokesman on control of the police, and his leader, Ken Livingstone, despite many good qualities, was and is an extremist. I did not expect to like Paul Boateng or to find myself in accord with him; yet I felt that I agreed with almost everything that he said. I am not sure if this was because he convinced me that he was right, or was just because he is one of the most brilliant advocates that I have ever encountered. The redeeming feature of May 22nd was the bond of friendship that was forged between Paul and myself which has culminated in Elke and me being his guests for dinner in the House of Commons after he became the first black member of the House. In many ways it was an inspiring week-end.

But it was also a depressing and highly disturbing time. On the evening of Friday May 21st I was in the dining room of Cumberland Lodge with three members of the Bar and we were all agreeing on the high quality of the fare provided. Suddenly a little man stood up in the centre of the room and shouted out: "This is the most disgusting meal that I have ever eaten. The chef ought to be ashamed of himself", and with these words Lord Vaizey walked out of the dining room. There followed a stunned silence, broken when José, one of the waitresses, came up to me and said: "Mr Crowther. The chef's packing up. He says he won't be insulted. You've got to stop him." It was the beginning of an important week-end and we looked like being without food for it. The chef was really in tears – tears of rage.

I told him that I could only assume Lord Vaizey had had some sort of a breakdown, and, if he would stay on, I would talk to the Bursar in the morning and try to secure an apology. I told him how his cooking had just been commended at my table.

"They say he's going to be the next Principal. How can I work for a man like that? He made similar remarks at breakfast," the chef said; but I managed to persuade him to stay.

I realize now that by doing so I probably thwarted the Machiavellian plans of Lord Vaizey, who would have liked the chef to walk out and was ready to replace him.

I could not find the Bursar next morning, so I spoke to the Secretary. Ruth was anxious, guarded, diplomatic. "I think that Lord Vaizey is going to take over as Principal. I am a little worried. He is – how can I describe him? Electric. He is here, there and everywhere. I came into my office on Sunday and he was rummaging through the drawers of my desk. When I challenged him about it he said: "You can't be efficient if you have to come in on Sunday and I insist on efficiency in those who work for me." She went on to tell me that Lord Vaizey had seen the Bursar and told him: "I can't stand you. I'm expecting to be elected Principal soon and when I am you'll be packing your bags."

Hugh Mansell had been the Bursar for about six years. He had left the Royal Air Force with the rank of Group-Captain following a distinguished service career and had invested all of his gratuity in a small business in Devonshire which had failed, leaving him and his family virtually penniless. It was at this point in his life (around 1975) that

Mansell, then aged about 50, saw advertised the post of Bursar at Cumberland Lodge. It offered congenial full-time work, a modest salary, and, most important of all, a home for Mansell, his often very sick wife, and their daughter, in the shape of a comfortable flat in Cumberland Lodge itself.

He applied for the position, was accepted, and worked there for about six years. But he had no written contract. When he was interviewed by the Trustees he was told that the job carried no pension but that, if his work was satisfactory, he could expect to remain there until the age of 65 when he would be eligible for the state retirement pension. It was, as he put it, a "gentlemen's agreement" with the Trustees. In entering into a "gentlemen's agreement" Hugh Mansell had reckoned without Lord Vaizey.

I managed to see the Bursar shortly after lunch on May 22nd and explained to him the events with the chef the previous night. I found him stunned and haggard. "Vaizey came to see me a few days ago," he said, "and told me that he will be Principal within a month or two and that we must arrange to go at once as he can't stand the sight of me. He says he has already appointed a successor. June [his wife] is sick again, we've hardly any money, and I don't know what to do. I asked him what I'd done wrong and he said: 'Everything.'"

In my view Hugh had done nothing wrong. Tall, debonair and aristocratic, he fitted in well at Cumberland Lodge, and cheerfully joined in the student activities, especially the Christmas parties, which Vaizey had already announced his intention of abolishing. Over the years we had got to know each other well, but he had always put the interests of the Lodge first as, for example, when negotiating fees for the visits of the students of Elke's and my school of English, or when banning Luvi our dog, after the housekeeper objected to his shedding some of his hairs. This was the man that Vaizey had resolved to banish in order to replace him with his own nominee, just as the chef had to be ousted for the Gardiner Merchant employee.

To me it all seemed most unfair, and I resolved to support Mansell, even if it involved fighting against Vaizey and his ambition to be Principal of Cumberland Lodge. That afternoon there would be a meeting of the Academic Advisory Board – the last that I would attend. At that meeting Vaizey announced (unofficially) that although there were other candidates he firmly expected to be the next Principal of Cumberland Lodge. (It was plain that a power struggle similar to that in C.P. Snow's book *The Masters* was going on.) I proposed a vote of thanks to Ruth Norton and Hugh Mansell for all the excellent work that they had done as Secretary and Bursar respectively in the last decade and this was carried with only one dissentient. This resolution was not to be mentioned in the minutes of the meeting. They had been censored by Vaizey. In fact, they had to be smuggled to me, for, after the meeting, Vaizey told Ruth that I was not to be sent details of any more of the activities of Cumberland Lodge, nor forwarded any further communications.

I had found the whole week-end most unexpectedly disturbing. It was Lord Denning who had introduced me to Cumberland Lodge, and he was at that time the "Visitor", which is a kind of trouble-shooter: I believe that a parallel office exists in Oxbridge Colleges; indeed, Lord Denning had been at one time Chairman of the Trustees. So it was Lord Denning that I phoned on the Monday morning.

Timing is the secret of much success in life, but one cannot always control the timing of events. I could not have chosen a worse moment to approach Lord Denning. In fact it was to Joan, his dear wife, that I spoke, for Lord Denning at that time found himself in a crisis every bit as severe as that facing Hugh Mansell.

I often heard Tom Denning laughingly claim to have "every Christian virtue except resignation" and I believe that our greatest Judge would have gone on giving great judgments but for the battle in which he had found himself that week-end. One of his many books *What's New in the Law?*, had recently been published. In it he had criticized the verdict of a jury in a case arising from the riots in the Toxteth area of Bristol, a case in which all the defendants had been acquitted. In particular he had complained of the numerous challenges to jurors – and each of the defendants was allowed up to seven challenges in those days – with the apparent object of packing the jury with persons likely to be sympathetic to the defendants. So the Sunday papers had got to work with suggestions that Lord Denning wished to undermine the jury system, was anti-black, and might even be sued by the jurors concerned for impugning their impartiality.

Well, we all used to say in my days at the Bar: "What Lord Denning says today will become the law of the land tomorrow", and shortly after that book was published peremptory jury challenges were reduced to three per defendant, and in 1989 they were abolished altogether. As for those who suggested that Lord Denning was anti-black, they should have seen him surrounded by Commonwealth students at the Cumberland Lodge week-ends that he had arranged for them; or have been in Mombasa with Elke and me when, following an entertainment put on for the Commonwealth Magistrates' Association, Lord Denning descended into the arena to shake the hands of every member of the African band whose playing had delighted him so much.

But this was the battle which Lord Denning was fighting when I phoned him at his flat in Lincoln's Inn on May 24th, 1982, a battle which, in reality, he was to lose, for the two pages in which he expressed his views on that trial were excised from all copies of the book not yet sold, and not long after he resigned as Master of the Rolls. Yet dare I say that I believe that he was right in his comments, and that juries subject to pruning by cunning defence lawyers are not representative of the British public as a whole?

Joan was kindly, diplomatic and protective. "You didn't know, did you, otherwise you would not be phoning?" (No, I had had too much to worry about that week-end to read the Sunday papers). "I'm sure you wouldn't wish to trouble Tom now, when he's dealing with one of the biggest problems he's ever faced. Please put it all in writing and send it to Tom and I know he'll deal with it once this is over." Joan was quite right of course, but days, valuable days, were lost and it may well be that in those days "the Battle for Cumberland Lodge" itself was lost.

Edward Clarke, Q.C., was an Old Bailey Judge. Not many advocates enjoyed appearing before him. He was meticulous, pernickety and prosecution-minded. I had known him since 1951 when I was just starting at the Bar and he was just starting to make a name for himself. Our relationship was ambivalent. We had frequently been opponents and I had often regarded him as an unfair prosecutor. The trouble with Edward was that he always wanted to win, and when you prosecute you should prosecute not persecute, as I have on occasions told prosecutors appearing before me. I think that it was because, as an ex-actor, he overacted that I usually won against him, and he was generous enough to admire me for it. As a Judge he almost invariably took the prosecution side and as I was always defending before him, fierce quarrels ensued between us. I remember one important case in which I was leading and had not only a junior but also a note-taker, and Edward behaved so badly that, for the only time in my career – probably to the astonishment of the jury – I walked out of Court, followed in solemn file by the other two barristers. Edward almost immediately called us into his room and was most genial: "Come on, boys. We've got a job to do. Let's forgive and forget," he pleaded pragmatically. A little later, at a Cumberland Lodge week-end this Judge, with whom I had more serious disagreements than with any other, told the students: "If you want to hear a good plea of mitigation, go and listen to Eric Crowther. He does the best pleas that I have ever heard."

It was during that week-end that he had invited me to go for a walk with him in Windsor Park. "What are your plans for the future?" he demanded. "I want to be a Metropolitan Magistrate," I replied. To my surprise he became very angry. "Rubbish! You'll do no such thing," he declared. "You'll take silk and then you'll become an Old Bailey Judge like me. You're ideal material for that. You mustn't waste yourself by becoming a Magistrate." "But that's what I want to be," I said.

"Listen," Edward said, and it was difficult to do otherwise as he was shouting. "If you persist in this mad idea and become a stipe, you will never become a Bencher of Lincoln's Inn, you'll see."

Later on I believe Lord Denning put me forward to be a Bencher because of my work for overseas students, But I was not accepted. Anyway I became a stipe and had been one for 14 years when "the Battle for Cumberland Lodge" began; and, unable to arrange direct contact with Lord Denning, it was to Edward Clarke that I unwisely turned for help. I went to him because I had succeeded him on the Academic Advisory Committee, and I genuinely believed that Lord Vaizey was seeking to perpetrate a series of wrongs which could not be in the interests of Cumberland Lodge. Edward Clarke in Court gave the impression of seeking to stamp out evil wherever he saw it; he could be a powerful ally, I thought. We had what the Americans call a "working breakfast" in his flat at Lincoln's Inn on May 25th, 1982. Edward listened patiently to what I had to say and promised to let me know his views. The only contretemps that we had that morning arose because I referred to Lord Denning as "Tom". "I think it is disgraceful that a mere Metropolitan Magistrate should refer to such a distinguished Bencher of Lincoln's Inn by his Christian name," pronounced the Judge.

"Well, he calls me 'Eric' and I call him 'Tom'," I retorted mildly, but Edward (or should I say "His Honour"?) was not convinced.

Our next working breakfast, in my flat in Lincoln's Inn, two mornings later, was a far less friendly affair. Edward arrived to give his reserved judgment. My involvement in a matter that was no concern of mine arose entirely from my personal ambition to become Principal of Cumberland Lodge [this was quite untrue] something from which I had been expressly excluded by Sir Frank Milton, another Bencher of Lincoln's Inn, to whom I was being grossly disloyal. Hugh Mansell was a hateful character and Lord Vaizey was quite right to seek to get rid of him. If I had the slightest instinct of a gentleman (which Edward doubted) I would here and now promise that I would never again set foot in Cumberland Lodge. When I declined to do so Edward stormed out of my flat, and we were not to speak again for many years. He did however think it right – and I knew him well enough to think that he did think it was right – to tell Lord Vaizey that I was campaigning against him (in my own interest) thereby giving Vaizey a considerable advantage in the battle that was to come.

When one has a serious complaint to make it is usually most effective to do so to the head of the organization concerned. Her Majesty the Queen Mother was Patron of Cumberland Lodge, but I did not think it would be appropriate to approach her, so instead I wrote to her private secretary, Lord Charteris, who was Chairman of the Trustees of St. Catherine's and Provost of Eton College, setting out the matters that I have recited in the preceding pages. I concluded my letter to him:

> "What makes the Lodge so special for students is the friendly, homely atmosphere generated by all the members of staff. I think this is in danger of being destroyed and if it does it can never be rebuilt.
>
> "The programme at the Lodge has hitherto been devised as a co-operative enterprise dependent on a great deal of good will. I do not believe that it can succeed as a 'One Man Band' – or rather a band in which the rest of the orchestra either says 'Yes' or remains silent for fear of the consequences. This is a tendency I have noticed in recent meetings of the Academic Advisory Committee.
>
> "May I ask you to acquaint your fellow trustees with the contents of this letter, and I should be obliged if at the same time in fairness to him you would furnish Lord Vaizey with a copy. I am sure that you will realize that I am writing as I do because of my own loyalty to and concern for the ideals and the future of St. Catherine's."

I have never met Lord Charteris, so it is difficult for me to pass any sort of judgment on him. I prefer to leave the reader to form his or her own opinion of the man and his involvement in this affair by quoting his reply to me, written a week after my letter to him:

> "Dear Mr Crowther,
>
> "Thank you for your letter and please forgive this hand-written reply.
>
> "As you requested I have given a copy of your letter to John Vaizey. I did this last night at the meeting of the trustees of St. Catherine's, but I did NOT acquaint the other trustees with the contents of your letter.
>
> "St. Catherine's is passing through very difficult financial times, and some difficult decisions will have to be made if the

Foundation is to survive. This is inevitably disturbing to the staff, and I hope that everyone like you who has the best interest of St. Catherine's at heart will use his or her influence to cool matters rather than inflame them.

"Yours sincerely

Charteris of Amisfield"

Meanwhile Lord Denning had invited me to see him, having received my letter. He was deeply disturbed by its contents. Reaching for *Who's Who* he demanded "Who is this pipsqueak, Lord Vaizey?" and, seeing Vaizey's many activities as set out in that tome Lord Denning commented: "I don't like the sound of him. Jack of all trades and master of none, I should think. I don't like people with long entries." (I have to admit that my own entry in *Who's Who* is lengthier than that of any of my stipendiary colleagues, and I hope that I shall not be judged by the same criterion!)

Then Lord Denning's sharp octagenarian mind seized on a simple legal point that I had missed. "He can't be appointed Principal," ruled the senior Judge of the Court of Appeal. "He's a trustee. A trustee cannot take advantage of his position in the trust. The Principal's office carries with it a salary and a free house. Lord Vaizey should never have applied. It's against the law. I find the whole thing most disturbing. I shall write to Lord Charteris."

He did, expressing his grave disquiet and stating the legal principle to which I have just referred. Lord Charteris replied to Lord Denning at much greater length and with much more courtesy than he had accorded to me, but he chose to ignore the point about the illegality of the appointment. A few weeks later Lord Vaizey became the Principal of Cumberland Lodge, and Hugh Mansell was ousted. About the same time our greatest Judge retired. Just before he left office Lord Denning wrote to me: "I am very distressed to hear of all that has happened about it [Cumberland Lodge] . . . I have spoken to several of the trustees. They all feel very anxious about it, but I am afraid there is nothing more to be done about it. I am very sorry you had such a stormy meeting with

Edward Clarke."

Sensing what might occur in the future I had asked Ruth to write confirming the booking for a long week-end at the end of July for Elke's school, the Cromwell School of English, and she did so. This had been agreed with Walter James, Lord Vaizey's predecessor, at the "student rate". Soon after his appointment I received a letter from Lord Vaizey stating that he had "been into" this booking and found that as the Cromwell School was not a charity he would not be justified in charging the student rent but we should have to pay the "full commercial rate". This represented an increase of nearly 400 per cent, and for the three nights that the students would spend there we should be paying out more than a quarter of the fees that they had paid to us for a 22-day course. I replied that a contract had been made and I should seek a mandatory injunction in the High Court to enforce specific performance of it. In reply I was to receive a letter from Douglas Wilson, Hugh Mansell's successor;

> "As you will know Cumberland Lodge has been passing through a period of financial stringency, and we have been taking energetic measures to reduce our losses. The Chairman [Lord Charteris?] has determined the dates of closure for renovation and staff holidays as part of the major cost saving exercise . . . and therefore we have been obliged reluctantly to ask a number of groups, including your own, to cancel their visits . . . as unfortunately the week-end we have for your group will fall within the period when the house is closed for renovation. I deeply regret this . . ."

If Douglas Wilson (whom I had never met) gave evidence and Lord Vaizey did not, and if Mr Wilson said that the period of our booking was the only time that he could get the builders in for the essential "renovation", and that he knew nothing of the disagreement between Lord Vaizey and myself, the High Court might well believe him, so I shopped around for other premises for Cromwell's long week-end away. The Chairman of the Cambridge Bench of Justices was Principal of Madingley Hall, a Cambridge University Extra-Mural College and a place of great beauty. Fortunately Madingley had a group cancellation at that time, so Cromwell was able to go there, at a charge very little above that which we had agreed with Walter James at Cumberland Lodge, so the immediate problem was resolved. The "renovation" of Cumberland Lodge did take place. It included spending an immense amount of the "stringent" trust funds on refurbishing the Principal's house, which Lord Vaizey re-named "Groom's Lodge".

My next visit to the Lodge should have been for the Lincoln's Inn autumn week-end in 1982, to which, as usual, the Inn had invited me. These week-ends commenced on Friday evening and finished after breakfast on Monday morning. Late on the Thursday afternoon, the day before the course was due to begin, I received at Court a telephone call from Colonel Bridges, the Under Treasurer of Lincoln's Inn. "Eric, I've just had Lord Vaizey on the phone. He had received a list of those coming from the Inn. He says that you are *persona non grata* and are banned for life from the Lodge. He says that if we do not cancel your booking the week-end is off and no student of Lincoln's Inn will ever be admitted to the Lodge again. He is adamant about it. May I ask you to withdraw?"

"You say he was adamant. Did he seem polite and reasonable?" I asked.

"No," Robin replied, "as a matter of fact he was extremely offensive, and kept swearing at me."

"Tell me," I persisted, "up to now who has chosen the speakers for these week-ends, the Inn or the Lodge?"

"The Inn, of course."

"Well, if he refused to have all our students Lord Vaizey would be in clear breach of contract and the Inn should sue. I intend to come."

"I understand your attitude," murmured the Under-Treasurer, rather apprehensively, "I shall ring Lord Vaizey and tell him."

About half an hour later I received another telephone call, this one from the Treasurer. I did not know Sir Irving Goulding, for he was a Chancery Judge, but he sounded (and is) charming.

"I have just had Lord Vaizey on the phone," he reported. "In my view it could not be right, legally or morally, for me to prevent you going to Cumberland Lodge tomorrow. We have made the arrangements with you and we still want you. I have pointed out to Lord Vaizey that he would be in breach of contract if you arrived and he turned our students away and that he would be liable in damages. I think he accepts that. But he says that if you arrive tomorrow or on any other occasion this will be the last of the Lincoln's Inn week-ends, and no member of Lincoln's Inn will ever set foot in the Lodge again. As our going there is really on a customary basis engineered many years ago by Lord Denning I do not think that we would have any right of action against him or the Lodge after this week-end, and I think that if you go the atmosphere for all of us will be pretty unpleasant anyway. You have always had the interest of our students at heart. I am asking you, in their interest, to forego your visit to Cumberland Lodge this week-end and for as long as Lord Vaizey is there as Principal."

"But he is younger than I am."

"I know. I ask you this with a very heavy heart, because I know that it is most unfair, and I hate asking you to do something that is unjust. I ask it simply for the students. If you insist on coming, you shall come and we'll see how things work out." "Did he swear at you?" I asked. "No," replied the Judge, "he was polite but very cold."

"May I ring you back?"

I did. There was no doubt that if I went there, generations of Lincoln's Inn students, many from Commonwealth countries, would lose the opportunity of a really happy and productive week-end with their Benchers and their Judges; I should be depriving them for years to come of the very facility that Lord Denning, many years before, had invited me to encourage. I told Mr Justice Goulding that I would not be going. I was to receive a delightful letter of thanks from him for my non-attendance: "I can only hope that your goodwill towards us will survive this regrettable episode."

The implications of Lord Vaizey's threat extended beyond the walls of Lincoln's Inn and the confines of the Cromwell School. It meant that I could no longer accompany the private schools of English or the Assistant Teachers. It was this last group, with so little done for them by their local authorities, that worried me most. The Central Bureau made it clear that none of their staff had time to arrange these week-ends for the Assistants, and if I were barred, these week-ends would not take place. Lord Vaizey's academic career as recited in his lengthy entry in *Who's Who* revealed a great deal of work for and interest in young people. Perhaps I should swallow my pride and seek a rapprochement. I therefore wrote to him on November 22nd, 1982 what I believed was a conciliatory letter:

> "At the meeting of the Academic Advisory Committee in May I thought it right, with Walter's retirement, to add a word of praise concerning the support that he had received from Ruth Norton and Hugh Mansell. I did not then realize the degree of hostility that you felt towards Hugh Mansell, but I had been shocked to learn of his imminent dismissal. I have, of course, heard only one side of the story. Hugh Mansell is in no sense a personal friend; I do not know him socially except in the Lodge, but I always felt over the six years or so that I knew him that he did his work honourably and well and had the best interests of the Lodge at heart, so I thought that he was being harshly treated. This view of mine has led to the only disagreement between yourself and me. The Hugh Mansell affair is over now; I believe that he has gone and has received generous compensation. I do not therefore wish this disagreement between us to continue.
>
> "If you would like to meet me again to discuss things I should be most happy to do so, either by coming over to the Lodge or by our meeting in London at a mutually convenient time. I have (I hope) few, if any, enemies, and I should certainly not like the Principal of Cumberland Lodge to be one of them; and I can see no reason why our former friendly relationship should not resume.
>
> "Yours sincerely,
>
> Eric"

The noble Lord replied two days later:

"Dear Mr Crowther,

Thank you for your letter. In it you allege that I felt a degree of hostility to Hugh Mansell and you talk of his dismissal. You will realize that this is a most serious allegation. It lay behind the astonishing action that you took in writing to Lord Denning and Lord Charteris of Amisfield.

"To talk of a disagreement between us in such a matter would seem to be an understatement. I find it astonishing that a person holding judicial office should expose himself to such extreme risk as you have done, and I must ask for an immediate withdrawal and apology.

"Yours sincerely,
Vaizey"

Once again I troubled Lord Denning for advice. Knowing how angry my form of nomenclature of the former Master of the Rolls had made his fellow Bencher Edward Clarke, I asked him if it was in order for me to address him as "Tom". I received the following reply:

"The letter which you enclosed from Lord Vaizey is most disturbing. I hardly know what to advise you about it. I rather wonder whether he is contemplating issuing a writ against you, especially as he indicates that you are exposing yourself to extreme risk. I feel myself that it would be wiser to remove the risk altogether and write to him and tell him that you did not mean to cast any reflection on him in any way . . . All this sounds very strange to me.

"Regarding your last paragraph, yes – please continue to call me Tom, as nearly everyone does.

"Yours ever,
Tom"

This was the only judgment delivered by Lord Denning with which I have ever disagreed, so I wrote again to tell him so. Lord Denning's many virtues as a Judge (and I write as one privileged to have appeared as counsel before him on several occasions) included being a good listener (a vital judicial quality, not to be found universally on the Bench). On this occasion he was a good reader, and I succeeded in persuading him to change his mind, for he wrote to me a few days later:

> "On reflection I think you are quite right not to apologize to Lord Vaizey. I do not think you have done anything wrong at all. In fact he should not have written to you in the way he has done".

Reassured by this advice I wrote to Lord Vaizey on December 10th, 1982.

> "Dear John,
>
> "I have been considering your letter of November 24th. I cannot see anything in my letter to you to justify the tone of your letter, nor to explain the change from 'Dear Eric' to 'Dear Mr Crowther', nor the change of signature from 'John' to 'Vaizey'.
>
> "I genuinely offered an olive branch, which seems to have been broken. Even so, the suggestion in my last paragraph of a meeting to resolve our differences remains open.
>
> "Yours sincerely,
> Eric".

I was not to receive any further letter – or any writ – from Lord Vaizey; I never heard from him again. Just before that Christmas, however, I did get a distraught telephone call from José, the dear old retainer who had been a cheerful waitress there during the two decades or more of my visits. She was clearly in tears: "Lord Vaizey said we were to wear Gardiner Merchant uniforms at all times," she recounted. "I told him I didn't like wearing a uniform and he warned me that I'd do as he said or take the consequences. Then this morning he caught me serving breakfast without my Gardiner Merchant cap on. He told me to take off my apron and leave immediately and never to return. I'm over 60. What am I to do?"

I advised her to seek compensation through the Industrial Tribunal, but she rang me a few days later to say that the Tribunal refused to accept her claim as she was only a part-time worker and over retirement age. José had been one of the staff who had always greatly enjoyed the Christmas parties. But all the staff and the students were to miss it this year because Vaizey deemed it to be "inappropriate". In fact only two members of staff survived the Vaizey purge: George Nolan, the friendly, ever-helpful barman and handyman, and Ruth Norton without whose industry and dedication the Lodge could not have survived, as Vaizey was intelligent enough to realize.

This sad year concluded with my receiving a Christmas card from Ruth. The message on it read:

> "I'm sorry that 1982 has ended with a cloud over Cumberland Lodge prospects for you. There will be no Christmas party this year. It will seem very strange. The Mansells have left, and the rest of us continue to 'learn to live . . .'
>
> Ruth."

Lord Vaizey's life sentence was to be commuted to three years.

When the Cromwell School is on, I accompany the students everywhere and we tend to get home quite late. It was nearly midnight one evening in July 1984 when we arrived and Elke gave me the news: "Lord Vaizey is dead. He's had a massive heart attack. I heard it on the radio." I should be hypocritical if I suggested that I felt any grief at this news, although I did feel sympathy for his widow, Marina, the distinguished art critic of *The Sunday Times*, and their three children. His obituary in *The Times* concluded with the words:

> "Although he could on occasions make enemies rather easily, he was excellent company, and, despite appearances to the contrary, he did not always take things too seriously."

I am afraid that I did not participate too freely in his excellent company. The comment of the Chaplain at the Chapel Royal was: "It would seem that the Almighty delivered the final judgment in your dispute with Lord Vaizey."

Almost immediately after Vaizey's demise Lincoln's Inn invited me back for a Cumberland Lodge week-end. "Who is to be the next Principal?" I enquired. "Well, Lady Vaizey is Acting Principal." I was informed, and so I decided it would be better not to accept. Later on I learned that she had applied to succeed her husband as Principal and, although I had nothing personally against Marina Vaizey, I decided that should she be appointed I would not return. However, in September 1985 I received a letter from the late Judge Bruce Holroyd Pearce, Q.C., a Bencher of Lincoln's Inn, saying: "The Cumberland Lodge impasse has been solved and we should be so pleased if you would come again in October, as there appears to be no outstanding problem over this."

The Trustees had not appointed Lady Vaizey as Principal. The post went instead to another of the many applicants, Tim Slack, a former Liberal Parliamentary candidate, and having seen him run in my "Bus Game" during subsequent Assistant Teachers' week-ends, I cannot imagine anyone more suited to the task – good-humoured, good-natured, intellectual, friendly and sporting. He and his charming wife make a point of standing at the door to greet everybody. But this welcome was delayed on the occasion of my return to Cumberland Lodge on October 18th, 1985 because as we drove down the fine long avenue of horse-chestnut trees towards the house I got the coach driver to stop so that I might take a photograph.

"Why do you want a photo, Mr Crowther?" asked the friendly bus driver. (He at least had not been changed, but he was not an employee of Cumberland Lodge.) "You've been here so many times before. Is this an historic event?"

"I would prefer to regard it as an occasion of triumph," I replied.

Chapter 5

Ornella

In *Last in the List* I recounted some of my experiences while working part-time for the British Council for 30 years. It was a bit (though being the British Council not altogether) like life itself: some of those I worked with I liked and admired very much; others I did not.

In the latter category fell Sid Vague, of whom I wrote quite a lot in that earlier book. But one aspect of his activities that I did not mention was his attitude towards girls, which I found despicable, since it involved taking advantage of his position as a British Council officer. Soon after his appointment he acquired a little "pad" about five minutes' walk from the Student Centre, to which he would repair nightly (and also quite often for short periods during the course of his duties) with his latest female victim. It was his aim, he used to boast, but I do not think that he quite achieved it, to get through girls from a hundred different countries. (This might not have been an impossibility had he been permitted to work there longer, bearing in mind the large number of students from all over the world for whom the British Council used to care.)

He came from a small provincial town and had, I think, a severe inferiority complex, although he had no need to have a complex about it. He suffered from extreme vanity about his dress and physical appearance, and was the only man I have ever seen wearing a codpiece, except for actors in Restoration comedies. The only thing that I can recite in his favour was that I never saw him lose patience or his temper with an overseas student – and this is more than I can say of some of the British Council staff.

One girl who succumbed to Sid's not altogether hidden charms was a tall olive-skinned black-haired girl from Sardinia called Marcella. Until she met Sid at the British Council Student Centre she had been a virgin, but that virtuous state was to end on the one and only occasion on which she visited Sid's flat. As with almost all his encounters Sid discarded Marcella as soon as he had had his way with her, and she felt degraded, humiliated and betrayed. Virginity was a vital quality in the rather prim and primitive Sardinian society in those days – I doubt if it is the same now – and Marcella did not know how to face the future in her homeland. Utterly depressed, she confided her problem to her "au pair" family.

Their reaction was extraordinary: they turned her out as though she were a leper. (She was "not fit to look after their children".) Distraught by now, and homeless in a strange land, she came to me in my capacity as student counsellor. She had about two months to go to her Cambridge Proficiency Examination in English, which she was very keen to take as it would be of considerable value to her in her work at a tourist office, so she did not want to return to her country, and in any case she did not feel fit to face her family. I was not using my little flat in Lincoln's Inn at the time, and offered it to Marcella. My first female guest there, she re-established her peace of mind in that atmosphere of tranquillity.

When she left England Marcella said: "Eric, I hope you will come to visit me in Sardinia. I have friends who run a small hotel in Olbia and they will put you up. You'll be my guest. You've been so kind to me and now I feel well and strong again. Come for as long as you like." People should not extend such invitations to me: I almost invariably take them up! So, finding that I would be lecturing in Genoa some time later, I wrote to Marcella and said that I would be coming for a couple of weeks, and she replied that I would be most welcome and she would meet me with her car at the port of Olbia when the boat docked early in the morning.

I always try to travel as cheaply as possible. I shared a small cabin with five swarthy Sards and it was pretty ghastly. The hot sun was already flaming fiercely overhead as we sailed past the town of Olbia next morning and I realized how far the port was away from the city. Eventually we docked and among the waiting crowds on the quayside I saw no

Marcella. I decided to wait on deck while more than a thousand Italians disembarked; still no Marcella. Finally officials approached and asked me to leave the ship with my luggage. There was still no Marcella but there were lots of unimpressive taxi-drivers offering to take me to destinations of which I had never heard. I decided to wait for a further 20 minutes, although I feared that by then all my would-be helpers might have disappeared.

I was feeling rather hot and desperate when a little Fiat Cinquecento drove up and a beautiful lithe blonde girl with gentle blue eyes stepped out and asked: "Lei è Mr Eric? Scusi che sono tanto tarde. Sono Ornella, amica di Marcella." Ornella, who spoke (and speaks) no English, explained to me that the previous day Marcella had been asked by her travel agency to prospect a tour of India and Sri Lanka for their clients and that it had seemed an offer that she could not afford to refuse; she hoped that I would understand: I did. "So," went on Ornella, "I will drive you to your hotel where we shall have lunch and then discuss your programme for the next two weeks. I hope you do not mind if I am your guide." I did not.

Lunch at the little hotel was an enormous and prolonged affair. The meal comprised mainly fish and shell-fish, washed down with several different kinds of local wine and Mirza. Over our repast Ornella told me a bit about herself. She was born in Varese, the shoe-making town near the Italo-Swiss border, but loved Sardinia for its scenery and its climate and had settled there, working for a property company for a very modest salary, showing prospective buyers over flats on the rich Costa Esmeralda. She lived alone in a tiny house in the country about ten miles from Olbia. The locals thought she was a witch because she did not have a man and they tormented her somewhat because she did not fit into their way of life, involving subservience to the male, but she did not care, because she loved the air, the sea, the sky and the beaches of Sardinia.

"Would you like to come to my little house?" she asked. "Why, yes," I replied.

"By the way, are you afraid of dogs?"

"Not at all, I love all dogs and they all love me."

"Skipper won't love you. She will try to bite you. She hates all men because she thinks they are going to attack me. The Sards hate her and try to beat her and I love her more than anything in the world." (Skipper, alas, was to be knocked down and killed by a car a few months later.) "She will go for your hands." "Then I'd better wear gloves," I said, and I did.

As we arrived Skipper leaped into the attack. Up and up she jumped, tearing at my gloves with her teeth, but although these garments were in shreds by the end of the onslaught, my hands were virtually unscathed. I stood firm and at last she tired and dropped down and I was able to enter Ornella's quaint, pretty, dark little house.

She made tea and we talked and talked, but as we did so I began to feel uneasy, queasy, positively ill. I still do not know if it was the mixture of so many heavy-duty Sardegnan wines, or the oysters; I suspect the latter. I had had oysters once before, while I was serving in the Royal Navy in Trieste. The first of my half-dozen I had swallowed down like an experienced oyster-catcher; the second got stuck in my throat, so I tried to force it down with a third. Oysters number two and three had a battle at the back of my mouth and I struggled against asphyxiation, while all the other diners in Ristorante Pepe Granzo looked on admiringly. In my desperate plight I was unconsciously holding up my fork while my elbow rested on the table. At last the coughing and the spluttering ceased as one of the last two oysters shot forth from my mouth and became impaled on the upright fork.

"Bravo, signor. Ancora!" cried the crowd of diners admiringly, and they started to applaud. I had no more oysters that night, but one (or both) of the two that I had consumed produced a severe attack of food poisoning that caused me to be admitted next morning to an Italian hospital for a week, during which I remember being nursed by a beautiful Yugoslav princess, a refugee from Tito's brand of Communism. Yes, it must have been the oysters of Olbia that upset me. I have had none since.

"Would you mind very much if I lie down?" I asked. "I'm not feeling very well," and Ornella put me to rest on her bed where I went to sleep, which was what I most needed. I awakened a few hours later in a cold sweat to find a body lying beside me. It was Skipper. She had decided that I was a friend of Ornella, and had to be protected. My head ached, I felt sick, I was shivering. Every moment I felt worse. Perhaps I was going to die.

Then I realized something terribly important. I must not die here. I must get back to the hotel to die. Sir Frank Milton was still Chief Metropolitan Magistrate at that time and he was very concerned about the image of the stipes. I could hear him intoning at the next quarterly meeting: "Eric should not have died like that, in that Italian girl's house. It's not good for our image. Let's make sure nothing like this ever happens again."

A worse spectre then presented itself: the *Sun* newspaper's main headline a few days hence: "TOP JUDGE'S DEATH IN MYSTERY GIRL'S ISLAND HOME" (You are always a "Top Judge" in the *Sun* if you might, as they hope, be involved in a scandal; even if you are only an Assistant Recorder who has not yet completed his first 20 days of sitting.)

The article would begin:

> "Flamboyant London Magistrate Eric Crowther, whose controversial decisions and eccentric life-style have shocked successive Lords Chancellor for years, ended his life earlier this week in an atmosphere of mystery in the bed of a voluptuous Italian blonde model and property dealer in Sardinia. Interviewed by our special roving reporter for European affairs the girl concerned said quietly between sobs: 'L'ho incontrato solamento quel' giorno' ('I met him only that day') while in an exclusive interview with the *Sun's* home reporter Mr Crowther's grief-stricken widow said: 'I don't know the girl at all. I thought my husband was on a lecture tour for the British Council."
>
> No, I had to get back to the hotel.

Ornella tried to dissuade me, but I insisted. She had to stop the car several times on the way for me to get out and be sick, while Skipper looked on sympathetically, but at last we reached the hotel where the proprietors gave me a large dose of Fernet-Branca following which next morning I was as right as rain (hardly an appropriate simile for Sardinia) and all set for two thoroughly delightful weeks with one of the kindest and most charming people I have ever met, a girl with a profound love of animals and completely in tune with nature. And I deprived the *Sun* of that form of obituary!

Chapter 6

An Incursion into Local Government

In an earlier chapter I recited the modern "Battle of Cumberland Lodge". Fighting what I believed to be a worthy cause I suffered what seemed at the time a defeat at the hands of Lord Vaizey as humiliating as that which Butcher Cumberland had inflicted two and a half centuries earlier on the worthy Scots, he being rewarded for his exceptional brutality with the Wardenship of Cumberland Lodge. To redress the balance, may I now tell the tale of another battle against corruption – intellectual, and not I am suggesting financial – in which I was victorious? This took place four years before the Cumberland Lodge affair.

At that time my wife was sharing a small antique business with a friend quite near to where we live. My sole contribution to the venture had up to then been to provide the name of the shop: "Memories of Mortlake"; I have always liked alliteration.

My knowledge of Local Government law and procedure is very limited. In my early impecunious days at the Bar Brian Calwell, the doyen of Bar lecturers, asked me to take over a weekly class on Local Government, which he no longer found it convenient to do, on Monday evenings. When I pointed out that I knew absolutely nothing about the subject, he said that this would not matter as the technique of lecturing was always to read one chapter ahead of the students and as these students did not seem to be reading the textbook anyway there was no danger involved.

So, because I desperately needed the money, I took the class on, with the result that in three months the number of pupils had dwindled from six to one and, as I did not like the persistent one very much, at the end of term I gave myself a fairly expensive Christmas present by giving up the class, from which neither the students nor I had benefited very much.

Appropriately, it was on a Monday evening in January 1978 that a Liberal Councillor in our Ward, Anthony Manners, called to our attention the fact that the following Thursday evening the Planning Committee of Richmond Council would be considering an application to build two houses three feet (yes, I mean three feet!) away from "Memories of Mortlake", which premises themselves include living accommodation, the proposed new building being of similar height to "Memories".

Why, asked Mr Manners, were we doing nothing about it? The answer was because this was the first we had heard of it. Although everyone else in the road had been notified of the application, Elke and her partner, the persons most affected, had not.

The next morning I was on the telephone to the Planning Officer, an official of Richmond Council paid for his services out of local rates, including my rates and Elke's. When I told him that we had had no notice of the application he said: "Well, you've got notice now or you would not be ringing me." I asked him to adjourn the hearing to enable us to instruct a surveyor to appear and he flatly refused saying that the matter was urgent. I said that I would be along to protest at the meeting and the Planning Officer said that I had no right of audience. Nevertheless, Elke and I decided to go.

We attended the Planning Committee meeting, arriving a quarter of an hour before it was due to start; plans of all applications for consideration that night were posted up on a board, with the exception of the one affecting "Memories".

There was, however, one empty space on the board. When a planning official arrived I asked him if this meant that the application affecting us was not now going ahead that night.

"It certainly is," he replied. "Who are you?" and when I told him he said "Then go and sit in the public gallery and don't make a nuisance of yourself or the Chairman will have you thrown out." It was not a very encouraging welcome to this first Local Government meeting of the former lecturer on the subject.

The space on the board remained vacant until the application affecting us was called on. Then the usher or whatever the official concerned is called, went and put up plans where neither I nor any member of the public could see them. Two Liberal members of the Committee did look at them, however, and one of these complained that they were inaccurate. At this moment Councillor Arbour, the Chairman, behaving like Napoleon in *Animal Farm* produced from under his desk what looked like a very attractive model of the proposed site which no one else had had a chance of seeing before.

Then the Planning Officer got up and argued the case for the granting of the application. In the short intervening period we had managed to get a surveyor to view the site and to write a letter of objection, which the Planning Officer did read out, pausing to argue vehemently as he went along against each point that our surveyor made.

Councillor Arbour, the "impartial" Chairman, said that he had recommended consent to the application "with reluctance" at the Planning Sub-Committee meeting (of which he also happened to be Chairman).

Councillor Manners spoke against the consent. He is a good man and a conscientious councillor but no one could describe him as a good speaker. (He has clearly never read *Advocacy for the Advocate*!) The Chairman paid marked inattention to the first half of Councillor Manners' speech, talking animatedly most of the time to the Planning Officer, and continuously and rudely interrupted the second half with political jokes, ("Councillor Manners must make the most of this unimportant little application because he won't be with us much longer").

After this awful charade the voting was even (writing from memory I believe four-four, but I am not quite sure about this) and it was no surprise to us that Councillor Arbour gave his casting vote in favour of the application.

Councillor Manners may not be a good speaker but he knows his procedure and he asked for the matter to go before the full Council. Anthony Arbour strongly opposed this, saying that their opinion would be irrelevant, and another Conservative supported him in this.

However, a further vote was taken and now there was a slight swing in favour of the matter going before the full Council. Even so, I left the Town Hall with sentiments of more anger than I ever remember feeling in my life after any judicial or quasi-judicial hearing.

I could not let the matter rest there. Four days later I wrote a letter to Councillor Anthony Arbour at his home address containing 11 (I thought) pertinent questions.

1. We arrived at 6.45 p.m. and were ushered to the public gallery. At that time no plan of the proposed development was on display, and no model was in evidence. Why was the applicant allowed to have his plan put up just as his application began, and why did you mention and produce the model of the proposed development which had not been on display before and which neither we nor Councillor Manners had any opportunity of seeing before the meeting?
2. Did you know the applicant before this application was made? If so, for how long and in what capacity?
3. What is the applicant's occupation?
4. Is he personally known to your Planning Officer?
5. Why, if as Chairman of the Planning Sub-Committee you recommended consent "with reluctance", did you cast your vote in its favour when the voting on the matter was even and all the speeches at the Planning Committee except yours and that of the Planning Officer were against?
6. Why, bearing in mind that the voting had been even, did you oppose Councillor Manner's proposal that the matter should go before the full Council and say that a vote on this issue was irrelevant? What was to be lost by its going before the full Council and why did you not want them to consider it?
7. How well do you know the area and how far away from it do you live?
8. Why exactly are you so much in favour of this application?
9. How would you react to a proposal to build two or three feet away from your premises (premises including living accommodation) a building of equal height to yours?

10. Can you account for our non-receipt of the notice of the current application (for two houses) otherwise than "gone astray in the post?" Was it ever returned to the Town Hall? Do you think it has anything to do with the application suggesting it affects only 39, 41 and 45, while 43 (my wife's premises) is in fact the most affected?
11. Bearing in mind "reluctance" with which you had apparently urged the Planning Sub-Committee to accept this application, may I have your assurance that when the matter comes before the Council you, in your intended capacity as a fair and independent Chairman, will put before the Council fully and fairly all points against the application (including the exact height of the proposed building and its exact distance from my wife's premises) as well as any points you can think of in its favour? I think you will agree that at last Tuesday's meeting apart from the reference to your "reluctance" that the proposal be adopted all your argument was in favour."
I concluded:

"I would not ask these questions, or indeed complain at all, if as Chairman of the Planning Committee you had behaved in a seemly and dispassionate manner, but I was incensed by your attitude to Mr Manners' brief argument; inattention to the first half, and barbed interruptions of the second.

As it happens I frequently sit in Courts and I can only say that if I ever behaved in such a way in the tribunal over which I preside I should expect serious complaints to be made of my conduct, and that is why I am making them of yours.

"Yours faithfully,

Eric Crowther O.B.E."

I did receive a reply, about 10 days later. It read as follows:

"Dear Mr Crowther,

I acknowledge receipt of your letter dated 28th January, the contents of which have been noted.

"Yours sincerely,
A.I. Arbour,
Chairman, Planning Committee"

I did not feel this response dealt adequately with the 11 matters that I had raised, so I decided to take the matter further. I sent a copy of my questionnaire to Arbour, and his reply to me, to every Richmond Councillor at home. Two of them approached me. Councillor Morell was nice, but his message was that what I was doing was damaging the Party – the Conservative Party. My reaction to that was: so what?

Harry Hall, leader of the Council, both telephoned and wrote to me. His line was different. Arbour and I were both magistrates and I was being disloyal to a brother Magistrate. My reaction to that was that if Arbour ever behaved in the Magistrates' Court as I had seen him behave while presiding over the Planning Committee I would regard him as unworthy to be a Magistrate. In any event, said Councillor Hall, only once in the whole history of Richmond Council had the full Council reversed a decision of the Planning Committee, so what was the point of going on with opposing the consent? My answer to that was that it was time that there was a second successful appeal.

The full Council meeting was a very different affair from the Planning Committee meeting. It was presided over by the Mayor with great dignity and fairness. Councillor Arbour spoke fervently in favour of the application and Councillor Manners spoke sincerely but not very eloquently against it. Then, when another Liberal Councillor, David Williams, a barrister, got up to oppose the application, the Conservative who had supported Arbour in the Planning Committee interrupted to assert that only one speaker was allowed to be heard against the application, a suggestion which the (Conservative) Mayor soon scotched.

He did, however, bring the discussion rapidly to a close – quite properly in my opinion – when he realized that everyone was speaking against the application, and he sensed (as we did) which way the voting would go.

Only three Councillors voted against consent being given. They were Councillor Arbour, his "winger" who had tried to stifle further discussion, and the only Labour member of the Council. I was surprised at this and telephoned her afterwards and she apologized and said that she had been tired and had accidentally voted the wrong way, something which struck me as rather amusing.

Anyway, the result was decisive enough to enable Elke and me to leave our second Council meeting in a much happier state of mind and to celebrate with dinner in a pleasant nearby restaurant.

But the odd thing was, as I told Harry Hall, that if Anthony Arbour had not behaved so abominably at the first meeting we should never have appealed! "I suppose," I wrote to the Leader of the Council, "that in an ironical way we should be grateful to him" (Councillor Arbour).

But Councillor Arbour is no longer a Councillor, although Anthony Manners is. Despite the massive swing to the Tories in Central Government in 1979 the Conservatives soon thereafter lost their control of Richmond Council's 60 or more members.

I do not know exactly what lay behind the curious conduct of this application. But whatever the explanation of his behaviour and that of his Planning Officer my point in resurrecting this matter more than a decade later is to emphasize that we should all think carefully before supporting arguments that more power should be devolved from Central Government, bearing in mind the power wielded by some Local Government elected members and officials, whether paid for by rates, a poll tax, or a Council charge.

Chapter 7

Ruskies

Peter Rusk was not a lawyer I greatly admired. I once warned him when he made one of his particularly outrageous comments to me in Court: "I am keeping a notebook of some your extraordinary observations, Mr Rusk, and if and when I come to write my autobiography there will be a special chapter in it entitled "Ruskies".

I could never understand why Robert, the super-efficient clerk of those respectable Chambers called "Q.E.B." where I spent my last six and a half years at the Bar, tolerated Rusk, but he always seemed to be hovering about the clerks' room. Surely it could not have been the gifts he brought to Chambers every Christmas: ties for the clerks and bars of Cadbury's milk chocolate for those barristers who would still accept his instructions. I was not one of these. I had one brief from Peter Rusk marked two guineas, the contents of which bore no relation to what the client told me when we got to Court. I told Robert afterwards that I was not prepared to accept any more work from Rusk, as I was sure that one day he would get a barrister into a lot of trouble.

I had my room in Garden Court, 50 yards away from the watchtower of Q.E.B., and Robert only made the journey to the annexe when he had some specially important mission to accomplish, so I knew that something was up when his small frame appeared in the doorway.

"Mr Crowther," he said beguilingly, "one of your colleagues is on his honeymoon and we all want to help someone in that situation, don't we? Well, he's got an undefended divorce tomorrow, and you're the only other member of Chambers who knows anything about divorce, so you will slip across the road and do it for him, won't you? I've managed to get it first on, and James has got your jury trial at London Sessions put back till 12 o'clock."

"All right, Robert, of course I'll do it," I agreed, before observing the grubby little bundle of papers not even glorified by tape which was the hall-mark of Rusk instructions.

"But, Robert, it's a Rusk brief," I protested.

"I know, Mr Crowther, but you have agreed to do it and I'm greatly obliged to you for helping out. I knew you would. I've spoken to Mr Rusk and he assures me there's nothing in it. I'll cut along now and leave you to work on it."

"Nothing in it!" I noted that it was marked five and two (seven guineas) as against the standard fee of 14 guineas for undefended divorces in those days, but one always worked for Rusk at cut rates. Rusk economised not only by not providing tape, which could result in loss of vital documents, but also by drafting his own petitions, which were invariably appalling. (This saved his having to pay counsel two guineas for doing this vital job.) Indeed so dreadful were Rusk's instructions that once when the others in our room and I devised a "spoof" brief from Rusk for Ronnie Bartle it took that experienced advocate several minutes to realize that the whole thing was a joke (see *Last in the List* pp. 247–9).

The undefended divorce was called *Iona* v. *Iona* and was a wife's petition based on her husband's alleged desertion. As I perused the petition I observed no fewer than 13 glaring errors, e.g. Rusk had recited a matrimonial order in the Clerkenwell Magistrates' Court before the date of the marriage, he had stated that there were no children of the marriage and then had asked that the wife should have custody of and maintenance for the two children, and the particulars of desertion alleged that the husband had left the matrimonial home less than three years before the date of the petition, three years being then the minimum period of desertion required by law. As I was seeking to unravel all this I saw Rusk passing the window on his way down to Q.E.B., accompanied as usual by his mongrel dog, which bore a remarkable resemblance to the cur that used to accompany Bill Sykes everywhere. I am very fond of most dogs, but I did not like that one: it reminded me too much of Rusk.

I rushed down and said: "Mr Rusk, I'm doing an undefended for you tomorrow. It bristles with difficulties."

"Nonsense," he replied. "There is nothing to it. I did the petition myself. Listen, I am Professor of Law in Leningrad University and I tell you that there is no problem at all with the case."

"I'm glad you think so," I commented, "because I want you there personally at the hearing tomorrow."

"But I have a very important case in the Clerkenwell Magistrates' Court," he protested.

"This is a High Court matter, and you will be there, Mr Rusk, or there will be trouble."

"All right. You are a very hard man," adjudged Rusk.

Because of the difficulties, I arrived early next morning but there was no sign of Rusk, nor could I find the lay client. In desperation I waited, and at about 10.25 the dog appeared, accompanied by a terrible Australian lady.

"Where is Mr Rusk?" I demanded. "I told him to be here."

"He's got a very important case in the Clerkenwell Magistrates' Court," said the Antipodean.

"And which of you is instructing me?" I inquired, looking meaningfully at her and her canine companion.

"I am, I suppose," she replied drearily.

"Good. Do you know anything about the case?"

"Nah," she replied in an accent that made the word "Strine" seem doubly appropriate.

"Then do something. Go and find the client."

This she succeeded in doing, and Mrs Iona stood smiling before me.

"Good morning, Mrs Iona," I greeted her.

She replied with something that sounded like "calamares", a dish which I like.

"Don't you speak English?" I asked desperately.

"No. Greek, Greek," beamed Mrs Iona.

"Have you arranged for an interpreter?" I asked my "helper".

"What's that?" she rejoined.

At that moment the usher bawled out:

"Number 1 in the list. *Iona* v. *Iona.*"

"Let's go in," I said. "Now, Mrs Iona, I want you just to say 'yes' to everything I ask you. We'll see how far we get before the Judge stops me from leading."

"Yes," said Mrs Iona, helpfully.

"And you," I told the representative of my instructing solicitor, "tie the dog up outside and come in and take a note."

"Can't the dog come in?" she enquired.

"No, one representative of your firm is quite enough."

The Judge was His Honour Judge Bassett, who would certainly not have appreciated the presence of the dog, for he was one of the most meticulous of Divorce Commissioners. I was surprised how far I was allowed to get with my leading questions, but the reality was that his ears were not taking in what was going on, because he could not believe his eyes.

"Mr Crowther." The inevitable interruption had come. "I have been looking at your petition in this case. So far, at a cursory glance, I have counted 10 serious errors. Has there ever in the history of English law been a more disgraceful petition than the one you have just put before me?"

"My Lord," I replied consolingly, "I think that when I was a Bar student the one I drafted for Bar Finals might have been equally as bad."

"Mr Crowther," he frowned, "this is no laughing matter. I shall give you until two o'clock this afternoon to amend it and get it into some sort of order."

"No, my Lord," I replied.

The Judge was aghast. "What do mean, 'No?'" he demanded.

"My Lord, I mean 'No'. If you will look at the end of that remarkable pleading you will see that it does not bear my name but that of my instructing solicitor. I warned my instructing solicitor yesterday afternoon that there might be difficulties and that he should attend personally, but it seems that he has a very important case this morning in the Clerkenwell Magistrates' Court."

The judge hovered between fury and bewilderment. "What are you asking me to do?" he asked eventually, in desperation.

"My Lord, I understand that you sit here every other Friday. I am asking you to adjourn this case back before yourself in two weeks from now, for I believe that it will take all of that time to produce any sort of order out of the chaos in this case. And I hope that your Lordship will not think me discourteous if I say that I have not the slightest intention of being here on the next occasion."

"Very well," said the Judge, rather sadly.

Outside the Court room Mrs Iona came up smiling and uttered almost her first words of English to me except "yes".

"I am divorced, yes?" she inquired.

"You are not divorced, no," I replied.

"But I give Mr Rusk all my life savings, £150," she lamented. (The average fees charged by respectable solicitors for an undefended divorce in those days were £100, out of which they normally pay about £18 to Counsel and his clerk.)

The Australian then made her first perceptive contribution to the proceedings: "I don't think Mr Rusk's going to be very pleased when I tell him what went on in there," she predicted.

At that point I thrust the brief (or rather the bundle of papers) into her hand and I said: "You may tell Mr Rusk that I never want to see those papers, or you, or Mr Rusk, or that dog again," and I left them all, including the most unfortunate Mrs Iona, in the main hall of the Royal Courts of Justice.

It was about 5.30 on the afternoon of the following Thursday week that I received a telephone call in Chambers from a very pleasant Pakistani barrister: "Abbas, here. Crowther. When I attended your lectures at the Council of Legal Education on Elocution and Advocacy you said that there was a long tradition at the Bar that we should all help each other, did you not?"

"Yes, Abbas."

"Crowther, I have just this afternoon received instructions in an undefended divorce case for tomorrow morning and I have a feeling that

that there is something slightly wrong with the petition." (This was the understatement of the Legal Year.) "May I come straight round to get your help in amending it?"

"Abbas," I replied, "in any other circumstances I would certainly say 'Yes', but if, as I suspect, the name of the case is *Iona* v. *Iona* I am afraid that the answer is emphatically 'No'.

I understand that Mrs Iona did not get her decree nisi next day. I felt that this poor woman had been treated so disgracefully by her solicitor that I reported Peter Rusk to the Law Society who, in compliance with their normal procedure, did nothing about it. Of course, if he had mixed any of her money with his own he would have been struck off, but the fact that he had overcharged her and taken all her life savings and had done nothing worthwhile for her did not seem to matter. But if the Law Society did nothing about it, my complaint galvanized Peter Rusk into action, and he came to see Robert, and this caused my Chief Clerk to make another of his rare visits to Garden Court.

"Mr Rusk says you're trying to ruin him, Mr Crowther," Robert opined.

"That's remarkably perceptive of Mr Rusk," I replied.

"Mr Rusk is a solicitor who has always been very loyal to these Chambers, Mr Crowther."

"That is not something of which these Chambers ought to be proud. I knew there would be trouble and I warned him of it. I will not accept another brief from Rusk even if the head of chambers is going on holiday to celebrate his diamond wedding."

For once I had triumphed over Robert, and no more of the many Rusk briefs which arrived in Chambers ever came my way.

Rusk's main hunting ground as an advocate was the Clerkenwell Magistrates' Court, where as a deputy stipe I sat in judgment for the very first time in May 1967; it was the grave misfortune of the two regular stipes there for most of that time (Frank Powell and Tommy Davis) that Rusk had his office next door to the Court, in King's Cross Road. Davis was not a man noted for his patience, and other advocates used to watch with relish the battles that ensued between him and Rusk. I was there on one such occasion when Rusk was leading an obviously guilty defendant through an examination-in-chief which was as irreverend as it was irrelevant.

Davis, who had been vainly gnashing his teeth for quite a long time, suddenly intervened with a barbed question, the defendant's answer to which pointed quite conclusively to his guilt.

"There, what do you say to that, DOCTOR Rusk?" he demanded with a triumphant grin.

Rusk as an advocate was always like a rubber ball attached by elastic to a bif-bat: he always came back for a furthering battering.

"I rely on the doctrine of *res derelicta*, Your Majesty," he rejoined.

At that the smile disappeared from the Magistrate's face and he started to growl: "That's a very dangerous doctrine for someone of your propensities, Doctor Rusk. I advise you to leave it well alone."

When in a tight corner Rusk, the advocate, had a habit of addressing the Bench in unsuitably grandiloquent terms. I think he was following the example of the Irish lady who, during Mass, always crossed herself at the right times but used to bow at the mention of the devil. When asked by the priest why she did this she replied: "Well, the future is uncertain and politeness costs nothing."

The future was indeed uncertain for most of Rusk's clients, but I think Rusk himself had a particular shock when he arrived at Bow Street Court on a Saturday afternoon in September 1968 to find me, now a newly-appointed, fully fledged stipe waiting to try a contested case of his. He quickly recovered, however – resilience was certainly his forté – to ask; "I wonder if I might crave your Lordship's indulgence for a few minutes. It may well shorten matters."

"Certainly, Mr Rusk." (I was at my most unctious.) "Anything to oblige."

I took advantage of the break to look at the summons and the information in the case, from which I gathered that the allegation was that Rusk's client had not been very well pleased with the service that he received in a restaurant and had punched the Greek waiter (I don't know why so many of Rusk's cases had a Greek element!) very hard in the face, making his nose bleed, and, not content with that, had taken up a table knife and cut the retreating waiter's jacket and trousers down the back, although fortunately the blade had not penetrated beyond the clothing.

By the time that I had absorbed all this, Rusk was ready for me to re-enter Court.

"Honourable sir," he addressed me. "I am most happy to tell you that this action has been compromised on terms that the defendant will pay to the complainant the sum of £30, the value of the suit, together with £5 for the complainant's costs, and that the defendant will pay my costs in the appropriate sum when I present my bill to him."

"Mr Rusk," I contradicted, "I think you are mistaken as to venue. You are not now in the Clerkenwell County Court where such settlements are commonplace. Your client is in the Bow Street Magistrates' Court facing serious criminal charges for which, if he be convicted, he may well be sent to prison, and I intend to try this case."

"But Your Majesty," adjured Rusk, "I was only thinking of you. It is a beautiful Saturday afternoon and you might be better employed on the golf course."

"Mr Rusk, I have played golf only once in my life. I was very bad at it, and I thoroughly dislike the game. Now let us get on with this case."

We did, and of course with Rusk defending it took hours, and was very dreary, and at about half-past five the defendant was pronounced guilty and heavily fined and ordered to pay £30 compensation and costs.

The only lively moment in the case occurred when Rusk rose to cross-examine the Greek waiter:

"You claim £30 for the suit. Why you claim £30 for the suit?"

"Because it cost £30."

"Look at my suit. I come to Court in it and it cost only £15." (This could well have been true.) "Why you pay £30 for a suit?"

I intervened at this point: "Mr Rusk, your sartorial standards for your forensic appearances and the price you pay for your suits, is of no concern to this Court. But if you are asserting that the waiter's suit cost only £15, may I ask you why, as a conscientious solicitor representing your client's best interests, you advised the defendant to pay £30 for the suit?"

A gem of a Ruskie followed: "In Russia we have a saying: a bad peace is better than a good war!"

In the early 1970s transfer between the two branches of the legal profession was greatly simplified, but subject to strict safeguards against the cardinal sin of "touting", and Peter Rusk became – a barrister! It was in this capacity that he appeared before me to make a bail application at Thames in 1973. I decided at an early stage that it was a suitable case for conditional bail, so I would spare myself the customary Rusk peroration on the rights of every free Englishman, Magna Carta, Habeas Corpus and *Woolmington* v. *the D.P.P.*, – it was usually a colourful performance – by remarking: "I am prepared to grant bail in this case if there is a surety. Have you a suitable person to act as surety?"

"Your Honour," replied Rusk, depreciating my value on this occasion. "There is a very suitable surety in Preston." I must have looked surprised, for he added: "That is a very famous town in Lancashire."

"But Mr Rusk," I inquired, "how can I be certain that the surety even if resident in a famous Lancastrian town is indeed suitable?" and I added, with heavy though probably unappreciated irony; "Has he been interviewed by some responsible and discerning lawyer – like yourself?"

"I must be honest with the Court," replied Rusk. (I refrained from any comment at this point.) "And I must confess that I have not personally interviewed the proposed surety. However, he has been interviewed by my instructing solicitor, who is a criminal lawyer of great experience, so Your Highness can be sure that he is utterly reliable."

"And what, may I ask, is the name of your highly experienced instructing solicitor?"

Rusk picked up his brief, (which I noticed had no tape around it) and replied slowly: "Miss Perrin" (I think this was the name).

"Miss Perrin!" I exclaimed. "Mr Rusk, I have been involved in the practice of criminal law for over 20 years, but I have never heard of Miss Perrin. From what address does Miss Perrin practise?"

Rusk resumed possession of the grubby bundle of papers and regarded them studiously: "149 King's Cross Road," he replied.

"But Mr Rusk," I observed, "that was your address when you were a solicitor."

"Really?" said Ruskie, "vot a coincidence!"

I refrained from asking if Miss Perrin were Australian.

My final encounter with Peter Rusk was at the last Cumberland Lodge Christmas Party in 1981, which I helped to organize. It was less enjoyable than its predecessors because of the Scrooge-like presence of Lord Vaizey, hovering in preparation for his take-over. Dear Ruth Norton rang me beforehand to tell me the exciting news: "We've got an extra student. He's a Russian Professor of Law." I was delighted, until I recognised him as – Doctor Rusk! During the Christmas Eve service in the Chapel Royal, Rusk sat next me and while the Dean was preaching Rusk kept disconcertingly shouting out: "What about Poland?" This was completely irrelevant to the Dean's sermon, but this hardly surprised me – a shout in favour of Afghanistan might have been more in point. However, on Christmas Day there was on the Christmas Tree a peace offering addressed to "His Worship, Eric Crowther, from Peter Rusk, Bar-at-law." It was a small bar of Cadbury's milk chocolate.

Chapter 8

Relations with the Lords Chancellor

One evening my son, Edward, then aged about 10, called out, "Dad come quickly, your boss is on television." I rushed to the set in surprise, for I had not thought that Elke had taken up a career on the small screen, but it was Lord Hailsham, and Edward was right, for independent as the stipendiary Magistrates like to believe themselves to be, and this is part of the joy of the job, they are controlled by the Lord Chancellor and his small department.

In my 21 years as a stipe I served mainly under three Lords Chancellor: Lords Gardiner, Hailsham and Elwyn-Jones. I always say that, of the three, Lord Gardiner was the cleverest and most perceptive – because he was the one who appointed me! In *Last in the List* I wrote that he had the reputation of being cold, retiring and unfriendly. To me he manifested none of these qualities: when Elke was seriously ill he displayed a warmth and kindness that I shall never forget, and twice he came to lecture for me on Sunday nights to overseas students at the British Council Student Centre (something that Lord Hailsham twice declined to do). I suspect that the greatest and most successful lawyer of my time owed his general reputation out of Court to the simple fact that he was shy.

Lord Elwyn-Jones had no such inhibitions. He was always friendly and outgoing. "Elwyn is all things to all men" was the rather unkind label sometimes attached to him, but I do not think that he was capable of an unkind act. As head of the Judiciary he had responsibility for, I suppose, getting on for a thousand paid officials holding judicial office working for him, of whom the stipendiary magistrates were among the humblest. Yet whenever by chance I met him in the Temple or in the street he would address me by name and in the friendliest of terms. He had this facility for remembering and applying people's names correctly, which I have often noticed in senior Labour politicians, and it means a lot to them. Elwyn was an easy Lord Chancellor under whom to serve.

I will say little of Michael Havers, a former opponent at the Bar and a personal friend for years, who, alas, was forced by illness to give up the highest judicial office after only a few months, or of Lord MacKay, who seems so energetic and so friendly, but to whom I have spoken only briefly on two or three occasions. However, on my retirement Lord MacKay wrote me a most charming personal letter, from which it was clear that he knew a great deal about me!

My attitude to Lord Hailsham is ambivalent. I have the greatest admiration for his scholarship, his intellect, his eloquence and his erudition, to such an extent that I would rush home in the evening to listen to his expositions and explanations on the radio of Greek poetry and philosophy, including recitations in the original language, with which Hailsham is so obviously conversant, and of which I am so woefully ignorant. All were delivered in that beautifully clear, resonant voice which was a joy to hear.

But it was Lord Hailsham who was Chancellor for most of my years on the Bench; indeed, he was one of our longest serving Lords Chancellor. However, he had little to do with the Stipendiary Magistracy; I do not think he ever met the Chief Magistrate except on formal and social occasions, and he certainly manifested no interest in my overseas students. Even so, I did have indirect contact with him early in my career at my least favourite Court.

Commencing right at the beginning of 1969, I spent 15 weary months as a Magistrate at Wells Street, a Court which, as I remarked earlier, I hated. One Saturday afternoon, however, was enlivened by the attendance of a defendant answering to many means enquiry summonses in respect of parking offences spread over a period of several years.

There was something about this elderly man's demeanour that convinced me that he was shamming: the shabbiness of his clothes was too calculated, the stick with the aid of which he limped into Court was too new, and the car, the parking of which had given rise to the offences, was too opulent. He told the sob-story of his long unemployment and other misfortunes very effectively, but I remained unconvinced.

"These long-outstanding debts must be a source of great anxiety to you," I remarked sympathetically.

"They are, they are," he echoed.

"So I am going to clear them up for you."

"You mean you are going to remit them?" he asked, a little too knowledgeably.

"No, I'm going to fix prison alternatives," I declared, "and once you have served those all this financial anxiety will be behind you."

"Now, it's £2 plus two guineas costs or seven days; and £2 plus 2 guineas costs or seven days consecutively; and £2 plus two guineas . . ."

The defendant's amazed gape became wider as the list of fines to be paid with immediate prison alternatives became longer.

"There," I said consolingly, "that means payment in the full amount forthwith or imprisonment for 182 days."

"This is outrageous," protested the defendant. "I've never been treated like this before. Do you mind telling me your name?"

I obliged.

"Right," he warned me. "I'm going straight to my M.P."

"And who is he?" I enquired.

"Quintin Hogg," he replied.

"But you have made one mistake," I said. "You are not going straight to see Mr Quintin Hogg. You are going straight to prison. You will be able to see Mr Hogg in 182 days from now."

"You're not sending me to prison," the defendant prophesied, correctly this time, for he produced all the money for his long unpaid fines from an inside pocket before striding sturdily but indignantly from the Court.

There was a sequel to this the next day which was embarrassing for both of us. I was walking in Richmond Park with Luvi, my Labrador, when I met this gentleman exercising his Alsatian at the same venue. The address in Marylebone that he had given was indeed in Quintin Hogg's constituency, but was the address of the defendant's retail clothing outlet. His home address was (and is) a large detached house just round the corner from us.

"I'm so glad your leg has recovered and you no longer need your stick," I congratulated him, as our dogs examined one another. But he did not answer and he still does not greet me when, both dogless now, we chance to meet in the street. And there are those who are silly enough to say that we should abolish imprisonment for unpaid fines!

It was some time after that – but well before 1982! – that I was at Cumberland Lodge for a Lincoln's Inn students' week-end at which Lord Hailsham gave the brillant off the cuff (or off the ruff?) opening address, after dinner on the Friday night.

"Questions!" he demanded, when he had finished, and none of the students present dared formulate one, so I felt that I, as one of the senior people present, should start the ball rolling. I forget what I asked, but I well remember the answer, which was:

"Well, ask a silly question! . . ." followed by the celebrated chuckle. There were no further questions that night.

I thought that I was the last down for breakfast next morning, but the Lord Chancellor arrived even later than I. *Faute de mieux* in the way of company, my being the only "student" there, he joined me with a cheery: "Good morning m'dearie" and indulged in half an hour of friendly, often indiscreet, conversation until his car arrived to whisk him back to Putney.

I served under four Chief Magistrates. Sir Frank Milton was certainly the most impressive and, always conscious of what he called "our image", did much to promote our position as "stipes" in general public esteem, especially among the lay magistrates, to whom he frequently delivered inspiring orations. But I think the friendliest of the four, and the most concerned for the personal welfare of his colleagues, was Sir Evelyn Russell, whose place I had taken when, as a barrister, I had moved to Queen Elizabeth Building. Whether it was this fact that caused him to take a special interest in me I do not know, but he was exceptionally kind to me, and asked me one day to go to have tea with him at Bow Street.

"Eric," he advised. "You ought to be thinking of advancing your career. You have sat for a long time as a deputy Circuit Judge" (since 1971 it was). "You ought to apply for the Circuit Bench. It carries more prestige – and more money, and so a larger pension for you and Elke at the end."

I thought about what Evelyn had said. I loved the work as a stipe and had never thought of applying to go higher (as so many of my colleagues had done) but there was a certain logic in his remarks advocating the inexorability of progress, and I knew that he had my best interests at heart, so I decided to burn my boats and apply.

A few weeks passed, and there was another invitation to tea at Bow Street. Sir Evelyn, who could look grave when the occasion demanded it, looked very grave. "I'll come straight to the point," he promised, as he handed me my cup. "You've been turned down. I can't understand it. I would never have advised you to apply if I hadn't made inquiries beforehand and been sure that you would get it. It seems rather unfair." (Evelyn was never a man to overstate his case.)

"Then what's to be done?" I asked.

"I think you should go and see Sir Derek Oulton," the Chief advised. "He's the Lord Chancellor's Number One on judicial appointments and we're all being encouraged to go to the Office and inquire about our career prospects. Ask him what went wrong."

So, late one November afternoon, I met Sir Derek for the first and only time in his little citadel of power in the House of Lords. I found him courteous, suave and urbane.

"Sir Evelyn strongly recommended you," he indicated. "There have been no adverse reports from any of the Courts in which you have been sitting. All the senior Crown Court Judges think highly of you. Those of your cases which have gone to appeal have never attracted adverse comment from the Judges of the Court of Appeal; quite the reverse, in a couple of instances."

"Then what went wrong?" I repeated.

"I don't know," he replied. "As you know, we need a lot of Crown Court Judges. I submitted a long list of recommendations to Lord Hailsham. The list came back with all the recommendations accepted apart from two names, which he had crossed through. Yours was one of them."

"Didn't you ask him why?"

"No, this is not the sort of Lord Chancellor to whom you put questions."

Remembering what had happened at Cumberland Lodge, I felt that I knew what he meant.

So I have never been able to discover the reason for my being turned down.

The Bar is, at present, a small profession and, like Lord Hailsham in his stalwart opposition to his successor's Green Paper, I hope that it may long remain so. Two of Hailsham's children are at the Bar. Both have appeared before me frequently, in the Crown and Magistrates' Courts. In their different ways both are very able advocates. Douglas, now a senior Minister in the Foreign Office, has some of his father's brilliant volatile eccentricity; Mary is much calmer, more subdued and more relaxed. Both I regard as my good friends. Hailsham is undoubtedly a very fond father and it is an extremely close family. If he ever discussed me with his children I feel sure that they put in a good word for me. They may know the answer to the question I have posed. But, whatever the explanation, I think that I have reason to be grateful to Hailsham, for I have enjoyed the rough and tumble of life as a stipe more than I appreciate the meticulous attention to legal minutiae that is required of a Recorder or a Crown Court Judge.

In fact, I came to know Mary Hogg better than Douglas, because when my friend and colleague Ronald Bartle was unmarried he went out with Mary quite a few times. (He is now very happily married to a charming Japanese girl.) Ronald is extremely good-natured and the fact that he never gets angry or takes offence causes him to be the butt of occasional practical jokes, to which I must confess to having often been a party. Hailsham's signature on letters consists of a huge letter "H" which is not difficult to imitate, and has given him the nickname of "Big H" among some of the Judiciary, so, during the period when Ronald was seeing a lot of Mary (also now happily married) and when he was also staying in my flat in Lincoln's Inn, I arranged also to stay there one night so as to be around when the post arrived in the morning, including a letter for Ronald marked "Personal and Confidential".

Ronald blanched considerably as he read the first paragraph, sitting down and sighing "Oh, my God." He recovered, however, when he reached the end of the missive. The entire communication read as follows:

"Dear Bartle,

It has come to my notice that you have been consorting with my daughter. Such conduct is, of course, quite inappropriate in a metropolitan stipendiary Magistrate and I must ask you forthwith to tender your resignation.

I have, however, no wish to be hard on you, and I am pleased to offer you instead the position of Chief Usher at Wells Street Court, with effect from April 1st next. Your place on the stipendiary Bench will be taken by Mr Peter Rusk.

Toodlepip,

Yours sincerely,

H."

Of course the news of this letter and its contents got around the four dozen London stipendiaries with the consequence that Lord Hailsham acquired a new nickname even more unsuitable than "Big H": "Toodlepip!"

People often ask me "What was the most difficult case with which you ever had to deal?" and I answer unhesitatingly "The Cat's Tail Case". I recited the facts of this disturbing episode very fully in the chapter on bail in the second edition of my first book, *Advocacy for the Advocate* (pp. 106–110) so I will only briefly summarize them here. In the middle of 1978, just after the Bail Act 1976 came into effect, a young man, whom I will not name for reasons which will become apparent later, appeared before me at West London facing two charges of sending noxious substances through the post contrary to the Post Office Act, 1953. Under the Criminal Law Act 1977, this offence had just ceased to prisonable in the Magistrates' Courts although the maximum fine for it had been substantially increased.

He had become enamoured of a young girl working in the same factory as he, but he was too shy to declare his love – indeed he had never spoken to her – but he found out the date of her birthday and sent her a bottle of perfume with an affectionate but anonymous birthday card. She opened the package in the works canteen in the presence of nearly a hundred other employees and roared with laughter saying: "I wonder what nutter sent me this. I don't like scent anyway." This remark cut nearer to the bone than she could have imagined, and the defendant, who was present, determined on a terrible revenge.

That night, with an offer of food, he lured a cat into the bathroom of the house in Fulham where he rented a room, drowned it in the bath, and then cut off its tail and sent it through the post to the girl at her home address this time, with an accompanying note saying: "I killed my Mummy and Daddy. Heh! Heh! Heh! Psycho."

A day or two later he caught a frog in the garden of his home and sent it in a registered envelope to the same destination, along with a note in similar vein. When the girl opened the package, the frog, miraculously still alive, jumped out at her, terrifying her for the second time that week.

Painstaking police investigations followed, including interviewing all 98 employees at the factory, and eventually the police decided that the defendant was their suspect. This was in the days before the Police and Criminal Evidence Act 1984, since when a solicitor would have had to be present at the interview and would have advised the defendant to say "No comment" in answer to all the police questions, with the result that there would have been no case against him. (The doubts that I was to express about the Bail Act extend to a good many provisions of the Police and Criminal Evidence Act as well.) But this defendant had plenty to say: his statement extended to many pages and included graphic accounts of how he had slaughtered sheep in Richmond Park and hung their entrails on trees there, taking two hours to tear the heart out of one unfortunate animal – inquiries of the Parks' Constabulary revealed that this had happened as he had said – and how he had at his home a large axe with which he intended to finish off the girl at the earliest possible moment because of the way she had insulted him. The police visited his home and found the axe that he had described. He was, as I said at the time, "a young man of insatiable cruelty".

The case had to go over to another day and the detective who had arrested him opposed bail saying: "I have not the slightest doubt that if granted bail he will go immediately to find and kill that girl." I indicated, perhaps prematurely, that I did not intend to grant bail.

But the young man was represented by counsel, who had been instructed to apply for bail, and had his duty to do. "You are bound to grant bail, sir," he pointed out. "These are now no longer imprisonable offences, and so they are governed by Part II of the First Schedule to the Bail Act 1976, which states that, save in very limited classes of case, of which this is not one, bail must be granted."

I was incensed, not by counsel, arguing his case firmly and fairly, but by a law which said that I had to set a young man free to kill an innocent girl. I did something that I think Courts should do more often and by-passed counsel to ask the defendant a very simple question (the answers to simple questions are often the most revealing): "Why do you particularly want bail?"

He looked me straight in the eye and answered quietly and impassively and with obvious sincerity: "Because I have to kill that girl. She has to die tonight."

"There you are – threats to kill, both in his statement and in what he said just now; and possession of an offensive weapon – prisonable offences," I triumphed.

But the wily counsel was more than equal to me, "The statement has not been proved in evidence to have been free and voluntary and will be disputed at his trial" – it was not in fact, for the defendant was ultimately to plead guilty to all charges – "and the axe was not being carried in a public place, and what is said in Court is privileged."

I was not sure about the last point and consulted my clerk, who agreed with counsel, and added for good measure: "You can't even attach a condition to his bail, such as that he should not go near the girl, under this new Act."

"Then am I to allow him to go and kill the girl?" I asked desperately.

"That is the will of Parliament," replied counsel, rather complacently.

In my anger I then made a most unwise remark: "Then if that be the will of Parliament, I shall defy Parliament," I announced. "Bail is refused. You will be remanded in custody for a week." Had I done otherwise, I should not have slept a wink that night.

Of course the Press and those concerned with the liberty of the citizen to do whatever he likes had a field day. "Magistrate Defies Parliament Over New Bail Act" was a typical headline, and *The Times* sensationalized the matter by commenting: "The Lord Chancellor will no doubt be sending for Mr Crowther to explain his conduct."

Lord Elwyn-Jones did not do so, but when I arrived at Court next morning at my usual time of 10.28 my colleague Peter Badge said: "The Lord Chancellor's Office has been ringing for you ever since 10 o'clock. You'd better read the newspaper accounts before you speak to them. I'll fend them off until you're ready." A few minutes later I was speaking for the first time to Sir Bryan Roberts, Secretary of Commissions, responsible for the appointment (and, presumably, for the firing) of Magistrates and later to become a very elegant and entertaining stipendiary colleague at Horseferry Road.

It was absolutely the only occasion on which anyone has sought directly to influence one of my decisions and so to interfere with my magisterial independence, and I am bound to say that Sir Briney (as I now call him) was completely correct. His message was clear: "Look here, Crowther, we can't have a Magistrate saying that he will defy Parliament. He's putting himself above the law. You've got yourself into this mess. You've got to get yourself out of it, either by granting bail or by finding some lawful way to keep him in custody. Unless he goes to a Judge in Chambers, you've got six days to find a solution."

I do not know why, but the defendant did not apply for bail to a higher Court – or, if he did, the matter was not listed before his next appearance at West London. In the meantime I did something that I would normally regard as most improper and asked for the detective in the case to come to see me in my room.

"Tell me about the cat," I asked. "Was it a stray?"

"No, it belonged to the old lady next door. She's very upset about it. She's made a statement."

"Good," I said. "Have him charged with causing criminal damage to the cat."

The officer looked at me as though doubting my sanity.

"Criminal damage at least is still a prisonable offence," I explained, and he got the point.

So, on his next appearance before me, I was able legitimately to remand the defendant in custody as he was now charged with criminal damage, and so his case came to be considered under Part I of the Bail Act, and I was entitled to refuse him bail under para. 2(b) on the ground that I had substantial grounds for believing that he would commit another offence while on bail (murder).

Towards the end of 1981 the Chief Magistrate Sir Evelyn Russell, the "perfect gentleman" of the Bench, said that he intended to retire, and for once there was no clear successor. Shortly after this much regretted announcement Sir Bryan Roberts called a meeting at Bow Street Court of the senior stipes, ostensibly to discuss "current problems in the Courts," but we all knew that the real object was to get to know us personally and to decide who should be Evelyn's successor, and indeed we reached a secret agreement that whenever someone was told that he would get the appointment he would immediately inform all the others, to relieve the suspense.

Those who were called to Bow Street that afternoon were, in order of seniority: Big Jim Harmsworth, the much-loved Duke of Marlborough Street; Edgar Bradley, appointed a year before me; myself; David Hopkin also of Marlborough Street; Bill Robins (who had formerly been my clerk at Thames) a most able and likeable man already sitting at Bow Street; and Peter Fanner, who had started his magisterial career with me at Thames, and not long after this meeting successfully applied to be a Crown Court Judge. To the best of my recollection Ken Harrington, senior to me and much-liked, was not there. Soon afterwards he retired and I was to replace him as senior at Horseferry Road.

Big Jim was a great man who did not really care for anything except being kind and just and having lunch at "Boodles", and he quickly made it plain by the flippancy of his answers that he was not specially interested in taking on the responsibilities attached to being "Chief". Bradley was a dry old stick, but a good Magistrate because he always seemed to come to the right decision and he was an excellent "Committee man".

Bill would in my view have been a good choice, having had a lot of experience of administration as a Chief Clerk, and Peter Fanner was also an affable and able "Committee man". The selection really did give rise to a lot of unusual speculation. *The Times* even adopted the rather undignified procedure of running a book on it! I quote from *The Times* Diary of March 20th, 1981 (of course, they knew nothing about our meeting with Sir Bryan):

> "Bradley will be the one to beat, though some fancy Eric Crowther (West London), another experienced committee man.
> The Times Diary betting:
> Bradley: evens;
> Crowther: 3 to 1;
> Robins: 4 to 1;
> Hopkin: 6 to 1;
> Bar: 8 to 1."

On reading that, Ronald Bartle, who knows nothing about racing jargon, felt that he was in with a chance (and he is now Number 2 at Bow Street, Bill Robins having retired shortly before I did).

Early in the New Year the phone at West London rang at 10.28 (the new Chief knew my habits) and David Hopkin's rich Welsh voice addressed me: "We all promised to let the others know, and you're the last one I'm phoning, for obvious reasons. It's me."

I knew what he meant, and forebore to correct his syntax to "It is I."

I was senior to David in terms of appointment, though not of age, and in the natural order of things would have been made Chief once Big Jim, Ken Harrington and Bradley had been passed over. I have never discovered the reason for the decision. It is probable that quite simply David Hopkin was considered the best man for the job: I think that he has shown himself to be a better administrator than I could ever be, and as Chief he has certainly always been kind to me: or was my name put forward and did the Lord Chancellor, now Hailsham again, simply once more put a line through it as he had done when I applied to be a Crown Court Judge? Or did someone look at the file on the Cat's Tail case and say: "We can't have a Chief Magistrate who says he will defy the will of Parliament"?

If the last be the reason I can only say that I have been glad to forego the honour and prestige accompanying the office of Chief Magistrate, the title that automatically accompanies it (and the extra salary and pension) in exchange for the letter that I got from the girl in the Cat's Tail case which read quite simply:

"Dear Sir,

Thank you for saving my life, I'm sorry if it's got you in a lot of trouble."

And I did save her life; I have no doubt of that. I had ultimately decided that my powers were not adequate to deal with the Cat's Tail man and had committed him for trial to the Knightsbridge Crown Court. There he pleaded guilty to all charges and Judge Friend, after reading medical reports and the defendant's confession (now admitted to be true) committed him to Broadmoor.

The law is full of coincidences. About five years later I had to sit at Tower Bridge Court when a colleague was ill and this same defendant appeared before me, charged with 23 burglaries. I recognized him immediately. The burglaries were all of office premises where the defendant had previously worked, all had been carried out at week-ends, all had involved the theft of trivial items like pencils and lipsticks and lighters from ladies' desks; the defendant had made a complete confession. He was "getting his own back" on women who had slighted him many years before.

My first reaction was to order a remand in custody for a social inquiry and mental and medical reports. A young woman probation officer, who had been in charge of the defendant on after-care, begged me not to do this. She had just managed to acquire for him a single person's council flat and was afraid that he would lose this if remanded in custody. She showed me a report from Broadmoor, where he had spent four years. He had been a model patient, except when occasionally he had become too attached to a lady doctor or nurse, who had to be moved on – Broadmoor regarded him as cured.

I was not sure that I agreed with that diagnosis, but I was moved by what the probation officer said, and I addressed the defendant somewhat as follows:

"On the first occasion when you appeared before me I denied you bail to which the law said you were entitled, and you have spent four years compulsorily in hospital after that. On that occasion I was not prepared to take a chance with you. This time, as a matter of law, I would be fully entitled to deny you bail, but I will take a chance with you. Please don't let me down."

"I won't, sir," said the defendant, "and I am very grateful to you. If you had granted me bail last time I would have killed the girl and now I'd be doing life for murder. I've got her right out of my system now, and she's in no danger. I won't let you down; I've got too much to thank you for."

I made a point of returning to Tower Bridge to sit early to deal with this case at the adjourned hearing a month later and, in the light of favourable probation reports, I placed the young man on probation for three years with psychiatric treatment as an outpatient (but with a recommendation that he should not have a female probation officer.)

The Author

Legal Visit to Moscow 1989

In China 1982

A couple of stipes on leave
(Ronnie Bartle to the right)

Cumberland Lodge

Together again: with George Nolan.
On the return to Cumberland Lodge

Isles of Scilly (my favourite place)

Ciao, Ornella!

I told him: "When we met the first time I hated you for your cruelty. Now I admire you for the efforts you have made to become a decent human being."

He repeated: "I won't let you down" and, eighteen months later, he wrote to tell me that his probation order had been prematurely discharged because he had done so well. He was proud of his flat; with the aid of the probation service he had got a job that he enjoyed, and, perhaps most important of all, he now had a steady girlfriend and between her and him there was genuine affection. I treasure that letter almost as much as the one from the factory girl he once wanted to kill. The reader will realize now why I do not wish to give his name.

"Non, je n'ai pas de regrettes."

Lord Hailsham was not a man lacking in courage. He was Guest of Honour once at a Judicial Seminar that I attended in a college in Roehampton. He arrived on his bicycle (his home is quite near). I happened to be leaving simultaneously with him. It was a time of considerable IRA activity in London. It was late at night and Hailsham got on his bike. A senior police officer went up to him and said, "Really, my Lord, I think it would be better if you went home in a police car. I will arrange it."

Hailsham's response was to raise two fingers and pedal off.

Chapter 9

Relations with the Media

Much as I loved Thames, I fulfilled a real ambition when in 1973 I moved to West London Court where I was to remain 11 years. It was a busy, interesting Court – any tribunal which has Kensington in its bailewick is bound to be a challenge – and it had the advantage of being near enough to my home for me to cycle there and back. One part of this operation was always rather precarious. I found that the only way to get through Hammersmith Broadway was, like Brutus's "plain, blunt man", to ride straight on. Once when I was adopting this tactic to cross the top of Fulham Palace Road on my way home a car "cut me up" (to use the unpleasant phrase so often used in Court to justify a subsequent vicious assault on the offending driver), causing me to wobble and stop in the centre of that junction. As I did so a police van pulled alongside me and the police officer who was the passenger addressed me:

"Excuse me, sir, but do you think you are in proper control of that machine?"

"Certainly, officer," I replied indignantly.

By now he had been joined by the driver who, coming close to me, asked:

"May I ask, sir, have you been drinking today?"

"I had a little wine with my lunch," I replied modestly.

"You do realize, sir," commented the first officer, "that it is a very serious offence to be riding a bicycle whilst drunk. And I have very grave doubts whether this machine is in a roadworthy condition."

The whole thing seemed to be getting out of hand but then the police driver, who had taken out his notebook, asked: "Have you a licence to drive this particular vehicle?" and it was then that I realized that they were two officers who had appeared before me who were having a bit of police fun.

And West London Court, despite the heavy lists and the tragic involvement in drugs of so many defendants, usually was fun. In the right-hand corner, as close as possible to the Bench, there sat every day John Hendry, the local press man, as he had done for the past 30 years. In the course of his service he had become a bit deaf with the result that sometimes he would come to my room to supplement gaps in his shorthand notes. I always obliged, and in return John would occasionally remark: "I got you down as saying so-and-so. I can't think you intended that. Could you tell me what you really said?" and I would be spared the reporting of some horrible gaff made off the cuff without sufficient regard to its implications. John was a great supporter of the Court of which he was an integral part, and of law and order – not a quality to be found in all newspapermen. Occasionally he would utter the dreaded words to me: "Mr Guest always used to say . . ."

Eric Ronald Guest had been the senior stipe at West London for at least as long as John Hendry had been there. He was a man of formidable intellect, surely the most brilliant lawyer to grace the Metropolitan Bench. Many thought that he would have been Chief Metropolitan Magistrate if he had not been so outspoken, a quality not encouraged by Lord Simmonds, the Lord Chancellor of those days (although he does not seem to have deterred Lord Goddard!) Others felt that his keen legal brain was more suited to the High Court Bench, that he might even have made an outstanding Lord Chief Justice. But he remained as the West London stipe, a man noted for his courage, fairness, firmness and severity, a Magistrate who did not suffer fools gladly; I was always surprised that I got on so well with him, and seemed so often to succeed before him!

Guest retired not long after I became a Magistrate. I think I was at that time the third youngest appointment in recent times as a stipe, the other two being Ronnie Guest and Nina Lowry, who also sat at West London – with me for a while – until her appointment as an Old Bailey

Judge. The reason for Guest's retirement from a job that he obviously relished was typical of his integrity. Young though he still was, he was beginning to go blind, and he felt that studying the demeanour of witnesses played an essential rôle in coming to just decisions. This he no longer felt competent to do, so he resigned (although an illustrious predecessor at Bow Street, John Fielding, had been completely blind.) This loss of sight was a particular tragedy for Ronnie who has but two other real interests in life, reading and painting. After I eventually took his place at West London he frequently invited me and my family to dinner at his home in Wimbledon, and very considerately always insisted that we took our children who, then in their early teens, were very proud to be included in the parties and made to feel important. Although many advocates who suffered the rough edge of his tongue would not agree with this assessment, Ronnie Guest was a good and kind man.

Even so, I resented being continuously reminded of his fine qualities by John Hendry and the clerks, especially the Chief Clerk, Ken Edwards, who was something of an eccentric extrovert. On one occasion I held there to be no case to answer and discharged the defendant after a long committal hearing of a serious charge. Ken, who had laboriously taken the lengthy depositions, obviously did not agree with my decision, for he ostentatiously tore up all that he had written and threw the papers on the floor in disgust – an unwise act, because if the prosecution had thought I was wrong they might have asked me to state a case and the Divisional Court could have asked to see his notes.

Rarely a day passed during my first two years at West London without Ken Edwards coming sadly to tell me that Mr Guest would not have done what I had done. I waited until Nina had been transferred to the Bailey and then when Ken came in with his usual complaint I said: "Mr Guest was no doubt a very great Magistrate, but that was many years ago. I am now Senior Magistrate here and from now on things will be done my way, not Mr Guest's." He looked deeply shocked by such heresy, but no one ever mentioned the Great Man of West London to me again, and indeed from then on Ken Edwards and I got on very well together and became good friends.

But with John Hendry as the Press Officer I was safe at West London from malicious reporting, to which some stipes and Judges have on occasions been subjected. The only exception to this occurred in June 1976 when I entered the Court one morning to see that John Hendry had been ousted from his customary seat and that the Court was absolutely teeming with reporters. I could not make it out. I had glanced at the Register before entering Court and had seen nothing unusual, so I just waited to see when the scribblers would start scribbling.

It happened when a middle-aged man called Alan Weekes entered the dock and pleaded guilty to being in charge of but not driving a motor vehicle with excess alcohol. It seemed that the defendant had had too much to drink at a dinner somewhere in the country, was driving back to his London home, realized that the alcohol was beginning to affect him, so stopped his car in the Earls Court area and got in the back seat to sleep off the effects before resuming his journey, but a diligent young policeman had roused the defendant from his slumbers and hence the current charge; not a very heinous offence, I thought.

Mr Weekes was very ably represented by his solicitor, whom I had not previously met. Neither did I know – or know of – Mr Weekes! The solicitor stated that Mr Weekes had been driving for over 30 years without any endorsement on his licence – not even a parking offence – and had never had an accident. He went on: "My client is a B.B.C. television commentator of great renown whose broadcasts give pleasure to millions. As he has to travel all over the country to attend these sporting events I ask you not to disqualify him, as he would probably lose his livelihood."

I addressed Alan Weekes thus: "You are a man who gives pleasure to millions and you have been driving for over 30 years without any blemish on your driving character and I therefore find it possible not to disqualify you from driving." I decided, however, that this famous man must be quite prosperous, so I find him £100, plus costs, and ordered his licence to be endorsed. There was an immediate undignified scramble to the only telephone box in Southcombe Street and suddenly the courtroom seemed strangely vacant – even lonely.

Only the *West London Observer* whose reporter was John Hendry reported my remarks accurately. All the nationals gave great coverage to the case, but found it necessary to abbreviate my observation to this effect:
"You are a man who gives pleasure to millions and I therefore find it possible not to disqualify you from driving." This enabled so-called "legal correspondents" to dilate on my "extraordinary" or "unique" decision involving a new "pleasure principle hitherto unknown in English law". One or two, really intent on causing trouble, wrote: "The Lord Chancellor will no doubt be calling on Mr Crowther to see him to explain his conduct." (Lord Elwyn-Jones did not do so.)

There is, in my experience of nearly 40 years of English law, no corruption such as exists in certain other systems. The nearest that any conduct of Court staff ever came to that evil occurred in this case. I rose at 4.45 that afternoon. (No one can predict when a Magistrate's list will finish; this normally happens when all his work is done.) It takes about a minute to get from Court Number One to the Magistrate's room at West London. As I entered it my private telephone started to ring. How many pieces of silver had passed for my betrayal, I asked myself afterwards, and which of my staff had received them? I never found out.

"Mr Crowther," said a voice as I picked up the 'phone. 'I am Harry Arnold of the *Sun* newspaper. I'm ringing you up because we like to get the law right in the *Sun*."

I could not refrain from commenting: "You do surprise me, Mr Arnold."

Choosing to ignore that, he went on: "In the case you had this morning of Alan Weekes, were you not bound as a matter of law to disqualify?"

I fell into the trap. "No," I said, "he was in charge of the car but not driving. In such a case the question of whether or not to disqualify is entirely in the Court's discretion." (In fact, on the law as it now stands, Mr Weekes might well have had a complete defence to the charge.)

"I see," said Mr Arnold. (He had seen all the time, of course.) Now he put the question he had really wanted to ask: "Does your decision mean that you would disqualify a coalminer – but not a Punch and Judy man because he brings pleasure to people?"

That was too much for me. "Mr Arnold," I said "every case must be decided on its individual circumstances. Good afternoon to you," and I put the phone down.

I was surprised to find that the case was the lead item on page one of next day's *Sun*, the article extending into page two where there appeared a photograph of a (much younger) Crowther opposite the statutory Page Three girl (the nearest I had got to one of those for quite a long time).

As a result of "an exclusive interview with the Magistrate" Mr Arnold was able to give readers of the *Sun* a lot of tit-bits, including the following: "A Magistrate is entitled to exercise his discretion, but this particular Magistrate has done so in a very novel way. . . Mr Weekes seems to be a very lucky man."

In fact if Mr Arnold knew anything of Court procedure he would have realized that nearly every Court in the country would have refrained from disqualifying in these circumstances.

This is surely gutter journalism almost at its worst, although Mr Arnold has since plumbed greater depths of degradation with an article in the *Sun* headed: "Queen Koo's Romps at the Palace". I am in favour of a free Press, provided that it is fair and honest, but I think that the Government should think very carefully before letting Rupert Murdoch or any other single individual gain any greater proportion of its control of the media, in which I include television.

However, I have never watched much television. I find radio far more stimulating to the imagination. It therefore came as a further surprise for me to read the following comment in the article of that great supporter of law and order John Junor (now knighted for his services to journalism) in the following weekend's *Sunday Express*:

> "Do you suppose that Magistrate Eric Crowther spends every Saturday afternoon with his eyes glued to the goggle-box?
>
> "I can think of no other reason to explain the extraordinary leniency shewn to B.B.C. sports commentator Mr Alan Weekes,

found asleep in the back of his Jaguar, stoned out of his mind . . .

"Is the same sort of treatment henceforth going to be given to everyone whose work affords interest and pleasure?

"And, if not, why not?"

When my son Edward, then about 13, saw it, he said: "It's a judgment on you, Dad. You know nothing about sport – I've never known anyone as ignorant as you about it – and every time we have the television on you say: 'Why don't you turn that rubbish off and go and do your homework?'"

After my experience with Harry Arnold I resolved never again to answer the phone to a Press man – except Tony Asciak. In my last few years at West London I did all the holiday relief at Marlborough Street after my delightful colleague Jimmy Cook had a serious operation which made travelling difficult for him, and just after I moved to Horseferry Road Tony came there too from Marlborough Street as senior reporter. Horseferry Road was a busy, difficult, challenging and interesting Court, whose jurisdiction covered about a sixth of the Inner London area – including Kensington, whose problems soon followed me there from West London. Tony, although younger, was cast in much the same mould as John Hendry, a journalist who regarded his occupation as an honourable profession, whose privileges he would not abuse to pander to sensationalism. He was supported by three younger men whom he influenced with his high ideals, and more often than not the four of them – "the four Horsemen of the Apocalypse" as I used to call them – were present in my Court, but they were always fair with me. I have had a "good Press". Once when one of the younger men reported in an unfavourable light a case of Captain Jobling which gave a sub-editor on *The Times* a field day and resulted in a quite virulent attack on my colleague on the front page of that newspaper, Tony expressed his disapproval to his co-reporter of his disloyalty to the Court – and to the cause of Justice.

It was the sub-editors who gave trouble. One of the worst instances of this occurred much more recently when I gave a talk for a women's organization devoted to the commendable cause of protecting ladies from personal violence in the workplace and in the home. I suggested that some allegations of rape arose from the regret of the morning after the night before. On violence in the home I said that when women made complaints under the Domestic Violence Act the Courts would stop all their other urgent work to give these cases priority, and often make an immediate order excluding the man on pain of imprisonment from the matrimonial abode. Then, a few days later, the police would arrest him and bring him back before the Court for breaching the order, but the woman would be there saying: "Don't send him to prison, sir, I asked him to come back. I love him and I can't live without him." So the exclusion order would be rescinded, and a few days later she would be back, battered and bruised, asking for relief again.

I said: "I am continually amazed at the patience and the capacity to forgive of some women, who can neither live with their men, nor without them. But it makes a mockery of Justice to blow hot and cold. We have to educate women sometimes against their better instincts."

A reporter called Anna Pukas really went to town over this, and the *Daily Mail* revealed "Outrage at J.P.'s Views on Women" and quoted a woman police superintendent present as saying: "If I had been sitting close to him I'd have put my hands around his neck" – a remark which, if in fact made, would seem to me to render her quite unsuitable for high police office for which I would have thought the quality of restraint to be necessary.

But worse was an alteration that had been made to what I had actually said at the time. The last sentence of my speech quoted above was transcribed in the *Daily Mail* so that the word "baser" was substituted for "better".

I have written elsewhere, in *Advocacy for the Advocate* (second edition pp. 142–146) of the efforts of a solicitor called Neville Kesselman to have me committed to prison for contempt of Court, an attempt which Lord Justice Ackner described as "the height of absurdity". Kesselman supported his efforts on his client's behalf by ringing my wife at home and asking her how she liked the idea of visiting her husband in prison, and his principal appeared on television to tell the world at large that he would do his best to see that that was where I finished up. When I complained of this to the Law Society, that august body found nothing improper in his conduct!

But the greatest shock that I got from the media came through the radio – and in the middle of the night! It related to the case of the Marquess of Blandford, who was to appear before me twice. On the first occasion the heir to Blenheim Castle, one of the richest men in the country, pleaded guilty to burglary and unlawful possession of heroin. While "stoned out of his mind" (to use Sir John Junor's inelegant expression) he had broken into a chemist's shop in search of drugs and, when his car which was nearby was searched, a small quantity of heroin was found therein. The Marquess, who had one previous conviction for criminal damage, committed whilst under the influence of drugs, was most ably represented by Richard Beckett, of my old Chambers, and ended up with a £1,000 fine for the burglary and probation for two years for the drug offence. Richard told me that the Marquess had finished completely with drugs and had joined 'Narcotics Anonymous' and was determined to help other young people to get out of the clutches of the most evil group of capitalists in our society, the drug dealers, who, bearing in mind the Marquess's great wealth, must have found him a most attractive target for their nefarious activities.

Johnny Horton of Narcotics Anonymous continued to ring me up every month to give me a progress report on his organization. "And how's the Marquess?" I would ask. At first the news was favourable: the Marquess was working with great vigour to save others from his own recent fate. But then Johnny became less enthusiastic: "We don't see much of Jamie nowadays. And when I did see him he didn't seem too well . . ."

At about that time I went on a law conference in Sicily and, over dinner, a solicitor friend of the Marquess said, "He doesn't seem with it any more. He seems quite unable to concentrate even during ordinary conversations."

Back in London I asked to see the probation officer who was

supervising the Marquess. (I think things might have worked out better if he had had a strong officer like John Smith or Geoffrey Parkinson to keep him up to the mark.)

"Well, not too badly," was her reply to my query as to how he was getting on. "He hasn't been in to see me for a few months, but he always rings up to say he can't come, which is more than most of them do."

"This is disgraceful," I pronounced. "He promised, as a condition of his probation, that he would regularly keep appointments with his probation officer, and he's not done so for months and you have done nothing about it except talk to him on the telephone. I shall have a warrant issued for his arrest." And I did.

The Marquess was picked up a few nights later in a cocaine den in a seedy basement in Paddington and on him was found so much cocaine that he was subsequently to appear at Knightsbridge Crown Court charged with having that drug with intent to supply it (a very serious offence). On this appearance before me he was represented by Monty Sherborne, another very able member of my old Chambers, who argued at length and strongly against a custodial sentence. But I had decided that the Marquess had grossly abused the privileges of probation and the time had come to deter him and (if I chose my words well) other equally foolish young people, and I gave him three months' imprisonment, a sentence which was upheld on appeal. The case hit the head-lines, of course; to the best of my knowledge it is the only sentence of a Magistrates' Court ever to be discussed in the leader column of *The Times*.

At that time I was suffering from a very bad back, and not sleeping at all well. I would often awaken during the night in discomfort and, wishing to know how far the long night had progressed, would switch on the radio. If the excellent "Today" programme had commenced, I would know that it was not worth trying to get back to sleep: my method of doing this is not to count sheep but to commence a summing-up to a jury. (The reader may think that if I do not send them to sleep, I bore to tears the juries I direct!) For my back I tried everything: physiotherapy, neck-stretching, osteopathy, faith-healing, having hot crystals applied to my back (this burned away my skin), acupuncture, and going to a man who looked and behaved remarkably like Frankenstein and to another who had started life as a butcher and had not, in my view, progressed beyond that trade. I wish I could remember who introduced me to Dr Wilfred Barlow, author of a book on "The Alexander Technique", for I cannot adequately thank that person for re-opening the door to happiness in my life.

Anyway it was during this period of pain and misery that I switched on the radio in the middle of the night and found myself tuned into the World Service. A discussion was going on between, I think, three people (one of them a priest) and a question which was asked early on caused me to sit up in bed in a state of horrified shock:

"Well, what we want to discuss is: was Magistrate Eric Crowther justified in sending the young Marquess of Blandford to jail for three months, and can a Magistrate who passes such a harsh sentence possibly be a Christian?"

I listened, rivetted, for the next half-hour or so as their views about me went out all over the world. The conclusions reached were that I was justified in law in imprisoning the Marquess, but the fact that I had done so proved that I was not a Christian. I did not get back to sleep that night . . .

In fact I am sure that I did the Marquess a kindness (although he has never expressed his appreciation, and for my part I have always, since then, declined invitations to functions of the Magistrates' Association at Blenheim Palace!) When he appeared before Knightsbridge Crown Court a year or so later the prosecution were prevailed upon to drop the charge of possession of that enormous quantity of cocaine with intent to supply and to substitute a charge of simple possession. After all, it was argued, the vagrant alcoholic will strive to get hold of just one bottle of cheap wine, while his rich counterpart will think nothing of stocking up with dozens of cases of Chateau Lafitte to stoke his addiction. Then it was contended that my prison sentence had been such a shock to the Marquess that ever since his release he had been living on a farm on a remote Scottish island to get away from the menace of his suppliers. He had now completely recovered and was determined to resume his good work for Narcotics Anonymous in London.

The kindly Judge Henry Pownall, Q.C., after giving the case a lot of thought, sentenced the Marquess to two years' imprisonment suspended for two years, so that he could go free. And so far as I know the Marquess has remained drug-free since. But Henry said to me: "It was your short sentence that cured the Marquess and changed his way of life. Without that, I would have had to have given him the two years straight, for possession of such a huge quantity of a Class 'A' drug." A practical Christian, perhaps.

It was during my last year as a Magistrate that I found myself in conflict with that powerful consortium known as Harrods. A young lady of 26, of previous good character, had appeared before me and pleaded guilty to a number of offences of obtaining credit from Harrods by deception, the total value of the goods which she had had during a period of a few weeks being over £2,300.

The facts of the matter as recited to me by the Crown Prosecution Service, defence counsel and the probation officer (for I remanded her on bail for a social Inquiry Report) were that she had received, unsolicited, at her home an application form inviting her to have a Harrod's credit card. It could not have arrived at a worse (or better) time: a music student, she had just been turned down after auditions by several orchestras; her social security had been cut; and a Lesbian relationship of quite long-standing had just broken up, leaving her with the whole liability for the rent of the flat that she and her partner had shared. In a state of great depression she applied for and obtained the credit card with an upper limit of £500 and, no proper checks being made, she went on a swift spending spree to the tune of over £2,300 – much of it on luxury food like caviare and smoked salmon.

Harrods applied for compensation in the full sum. Under the Criminal Justice Act 1988, if a Court does not order compensation it has to give its reasons in open Court. This is what, in sentencing the defendant to 60 hours Community Service, I said:

"You received this card uninvited, allowing you the most valuable credit from the most expensive store in London. And you got this thrill because nobody made a proper check. If they had done so they would have realized that there was no money in your bank account.

"Harrods is the author of its own misfortune. It blatantly encourages people to live on credit, which is extremely undesirable and brought about by their greed in getting people to buy their goods in every manner possible. More cogent than that, considering your income, which is less than £34 a week, and that you have a bank overdraft of £300, I consider it wholly impractical to order you to pay compensation."

"Magistrate Condemns Greedy Harrods" was the favourite newspaper headline, and Mr Michael Cole (late of the B.B.C.) now Harrods' "media director" went on television to say that the Al Fayed Brothers had been "deeply hurt" and "extremely concerned" by my "unhelpful, unjustified and unfair remarks". (One can imagine them crying all the way back from the credit bank.) He went on to complain that: (i) Harrods never sent unsolicited applications for credit cards through the post; (ii) that when applying for the credit card the defendant had used the name and address of her mother, in Yorkshire, and had forged her mother's signature.

These complaints were repeated in a letter of complaint by Harrods' solicitor, a Mr Chambers, to Lord MacKay, the Lord Chancellor, to which I was required to reply.

As to the first of Harrods' contentions, many students at International Students' House, where I do voluntary work, told me that they had received application forms unsolicited through the post from Harrods; and Mary Asprey, a neighbour and good friend (wife of one of the brothers Asprey, jewellers of Bond Street) said that she had also recently received one in similar circumstances. Before making my criticism of Harrods I had asked the Crown Prosecution Service representative: "Did this application invitation just arrive through the post, out of the blue?" and she replied "Yes"; and I believe that was the case. The defendant had said this to the police, to her solicitor and to the Probation Officer.

The second complaint by Harrods had more substance, for I was never told by the C.P.S. (as was the case) that the girl when making her application had given her mother's details and her mother's bank account. The deception of which I was informed was that she had given the Christian name of Joan (but her own surname) and had stated that she was employed, while she was not. However, it seems to me that if Harrods had made proper checks on the mother and her bank account they would immediately have discovered the true facts, for there was no suggestion that the mother, 200 miles away, was a party to this fraud. I therefore stand by my contention that Harrods were the authors of their own misfortune.

The letter that I wrote to the Lord Chancellor's Department was full of irony. If indeed Harrods had been "deeply hurt" and were "extremely concerned" by my remarks it was a matter of great regret to me, I said, and my comments were faithfully and properly reported by an official of the Lord Chancellor's Department when writing to Harrods. But their representation of all this to the Press adopted a different slant, implying that I had made an abject apology (the irony was omitted) and a typical headline which I was amazed to read on my way out to Italy on leave was that in the *Evening Standard*: "Victory for Harrods in Credit Row".

The affair had its funny side, however, and among the many communications that I received on the subject were two which I now quote. The first, written in a childish hand, must be attributed to one of the wittier of my colleagues:

> "Dear Mr Crowther,
>
> My Daddy was very pleesed when you said that Harrods were gready and made people spend too much money which they didn't have jus like my Mummy always does.
>
> "He says please will you say the same about Peter Jones and Selfrijis where she also spends lotsa money and while you're at it would you say it about Visa and Akcess and American Express.
>
> "Please say these things becos it made Daddy so pleesed he

gave me some sweets.

"Yors sincerely

"Anna Black (aged seven)

"P.S. My Daddy is also a stipeniury Magistrate but he never gets interestink cases like you. He only does some specialy boring cases called Frigging Road Traffic Again."

I never discovered where the other one came from. It was a formal invitation card and read:

"Johnny Al Fayed
of
Harrods
invites
Eric Crowther, O.B.E., J.P.
TO THE LAUNCH OF THEIR NEW 'ARISTOCARD'
11 years* interest free charge card
1900 hours Friday 13th January
Bring a bottle (full)

**Applications accepted from children of three upwards, J.P.s need not apply."*

For many years I was Chairman of the Committee in charge of the training of new Justices in Inner London. One of the precepts that I always advanced to them was: "If the defendant has committed another prisonable offence whilst subject to a suspended sentence he must go to prison; otherwise you are sitting as an unofficial Court of Appeal from your colleagues." But in my last month as a Magistrate (September 1989) I am afraid that I broke this rule.

The defendant was a middle-aged man whose occupation could properly be described as "shoplifter". About ten days earlier he had pleaded guilty to stealing a single item from Harrods and had been sentenced by the lay justices at Horseferry Road to six months' imprisonment suspended for two years. In case that sentence should seem harsh, I ought to point out that it was his 57th conviction for shoplifting at our Court that year, and on none of the others had any Court passed a sentence of imprisonment, either immediate or suspended. For the most part he had been dealt with by fines, all of which remained unpaid; and there are those who complain that Magistrates are too ready to commit defendants to prison!

On this occasion the defendant pleaded guilty to the charge as put to him by the learned clerk: "That yesterday, at Harrods, you stole one tee-shirt to the value of £435." "What, £435 for a tee-shirt?" I could not restrain myself from expostulating.

The Crown Prosecution Service was in good form that day. Not only did they have the papers with them; they also had the exhibit. "I have the garment here, sir, if you would care to see it," offered the charming girl who represented the Crown.

"I not only want to see it, I want to handle it," I exclaimed (I used the word "handle" in the non-legal sense of the term). "It must be made of gossamer, if it's worth £435."

A flimsy little piece of material was then handed up to me, and I could not fail to observe the label "Made in Taiwan" as I dropped it contemptuously on the Bench before me, at the same time declaring: "Well, I wouldn't give anybody £435 for that!"

"That's exactly what I thought, guv'nor!" rejoined the defendant.

Well, I could not send him to prison after repartee as brilliant as that: the public in the gallery would not have been with me, and you have got to carry along with you the local people whom, as a Magistrate, you represent. Instead I deferred sentence for six months to see if the defendant could keep out of trouble; but I think that Harrods must have been quite glad when I retired . . .

Chapter 10

Relations with the Public

In 1937 the Chairman of the Magistrates' Association protested to Lord Reith, the Director-General of the B.B.C., that a sketch on the radio entitled "Mr Muddlecombe, J.P.", performed by Robb Wilton, had impugned the dignity of the magistracy, and the Chairman went on to threaten to report the matter to the Home Secretary, if there were no apology. None was forthcoming from Lord Reith who, to his credit, found the matter "ludicrous and fantastic". Robb Wilton's comment was "If you can't burlesque the Magistrates, whom on earth can you burlesque?"

During 40 years in the law I have never come across a Judge or a Magistrate who was corrupt, I have met only one or two whom I thought stupid, a very slightly larger number who lacked feeling and sensitivity, and an awful lot who were pompous; the last is a characteristic much to be eschewed by all in authority, from policemen to High Court Judges.

It is very important when sitting on the Bench not to get angry over trivia. Stephen Dawson, a very able solicitor who often appeared before me, reminded me recently of an incident that occurred about three years earlier at Horseferry Road and which I had forgotten. The defendant was a young undergraduate charged with an offence under the Public Order Act arising from a student demonstration. The Clerk asked the defendant to stand while he put the charge.

"No," said the young intellectual. "The Magistrate is sitting and we are all equal in law and so I see no reason why I should not be on the same level as he."

I then got up from my seat and said: "Well, in that case I shall stand while the charge is read." The defendant looked a bit perplexed, but then rose to his feet. After the charge had been put and he had pleaded guilty I asked him: "Shall we both sit down now?" and he agreed and we did, and there were no more procedural difficulties. He was a young man of good character (if one excludes the offence of arrogance) and went away quite happy with his conditional discharge.

Others on similar charges can be more difficult. A pretty young "Greenham Common" woman, who gave her name as Kitty Blue, had hurled herself in front of President Reagan's car as it attempted to enter the grounds of Buckingham Palace for the President to have dinner with Her Majesty the Queen. Understandably she was arrested for obstruction; less understandably she pleaded Not Guilty, being desirous of making public political statements against atomic weapons and the presence of American soldiers in Britain. She sacked her lawyer at the beginning of the case, then asked to have the services of a "Mackenzie man" to assist her throughout the trial; between them they managed to make the case last until after 5 o'clock, but throughout it was conducted with patience from the Bench, and courtesy on the part of the defendant and her unofficial advisor.

At the end of this marathon I convicted her. "Well," she said defiantly, "you might as well imprison me right away because I warn you I shan't pay any fine and I won't accept probation or a bind over."

"I am not going to be so severe on you," I commented. "I think this was silly rather than serious. You will be discharged on condition of good behaviour for a year."

"I don't accept it," she shouted, "I want to go to prison."

"I'm afraid you'll have to accept it," I replied. "A conditional discharge does not require your consent."

A hard glint came to her attractive eyes as she furrowed her brow. "I thought you were quite nice during the trial," she adjudged, "but now I realize you're a real bastard."

On a Sunday morning in 1973 a dock worker left his Jaguar car parked on a double yellow line in Middlesex Street, E1. This was a foolish thing to do because on Sunday mornings Middlesex Street becomes

Petticoat Lane, one of the busiest open-air markets in the world, and when the stevedore returned to his vehicle he found a policeman there writing out a ticket. He was not pleased, and reacted with: "You bloody coppers. You're all the bloody same. Can't you find anything better to bloody well do than persecute us poor bloody dockers."

"Well, if that's your attitude," responded the policeman, rising up on his toes, "I'll have you for obscene language as well" And he did, for next morning the errant motorist appeared before me at Thames and pleaded guilty to two charges: unnecessary obstruction, and "using obscene language to the annoyance of passengers" (by which is meant passers-by).

All this happened in the halcyon days when there appeared before the Court the police officer in the case, who knew all about it; now the facts are presented by a representative of the Crown Prosecution Service, who if he (and the Court) is lucky reads from a set of badly written papers that he has just received – but quite often the police have not delivered the papers . . .

"Is that all he said?" I asked the policeman, and, on getting an affirmative reply, I reopened the case, advised the defendant to plead Not Guilty to the obscene language charge, heard it there and then (it took only about 10 minutes) and acquitted him. In giving judgment I said: "When Bernard Shaw got Eliza Doolittle to say: 'Not bloody likely' in *Pygmalion* 40 years or so ago, British society was outraged, but last night I watched a play on television in which that epithet was used at least six times. If it is permissable to say it to millions of people in their homes, I fail to see why it is a crime to say it to one policeman, who really must be used to hearing such language as part of his job and in the police canteen. There has been no evidence that any passer-by was affected by the utterance."

All the main British newspapers carried the item concerning the Magistrate's "controversial" decision, and I achieved fame in the *New York Times*, which, with typical American hyberbole, gave it the banner headline: "ENGLISH JUDGE RULES 'BLOODY' O.K." During the next few days I received 97 letters on the subject from members of the public, all of which were hostile, many of which contained personal abuse, while one or two were, in my opinion, themselves obscene. Of these I decided to answer only one, which read:

> "I am an old-age pensioner and all my life I have been a God-fearing Methodist, brought up to believe in the goodness of the law. I feel that you have let down the high standards in which I have always believed, and I am disappointed in you."

This one I felt required a reply, so I wrote to this worthy gentleman saying, as is the fact, that I do not myself engage in bad language, which I regard as a substitute for meaningful expression – one of my correspondents had alleged that obviously I used such language all the time to my children – but that, apart from the question whether "bloody" was still to be regarded as obscene, there was the further element that the language had to be used "to the annoyance of passengers" (in the plural) and there had been no evidence that anyone passing by had been annoyed except the solitary policeman, whose back ought to be broad enough to bear it anyway. (This was, I think, a correct statement of the law at the time, although recent decisions of the Divisional Court in cases brought under the Public Order Act 1986 indicate that a policeman can be as sensitive as the rest of us.)

The old boy wrote back to me saying that his faith in English law had been restored, and we continued to send each other Christmas cards until about three years ago when I received a letter from his sister saying that he had recently died, still, I hope, believing in British justice.

But the "Bloody Docker" case illustrates a strange feature of the British character. People will readily write to the Judge or Magistrate (or, worse still, to the Press) to say that judicial decisions are wrong, but very rarely, if ever, are they moved to say that the Judge was right. And yet I do not believe that all my verdicts have been wrong. A matter that attracted great publicity was my decision to grant bail to Michael Groce, a man with a formidable criminal record, facing a charge of armed robbery. I granted bail because, when armed police went to arrest him and he, unarmed, hearing them, moved suddenly, a police inspector fired a shot which permanently crippled Groce's blameless mother, who in consequence was lying critically ill in hospital. Groce was most ably represented by Paul Boateng, who convinced me that the defendant and his mother were devoted to each other, and it would be a tragedy if she died without seeing him again. Groce's grandmother, a most formidable and devout Seventh Day Adventist, offered herself as a surety, and I granted him bail on terms that he should reside with his grandmother (as stern an individual as any prison warder I have ever met) and leave her house only in her company to visit his mother in hospital – the first instance of "House Arrest" in this country, as I called it. I have no doubt that this decision to grant bail, based mostly on compassion, was right: it was surely proved to be so when subsequently the police offered no evidence against Groce on the armed robbery charge. Yet nobody wrote to me about that decision, although later on a superintendent of police did congratulate me, saying: "The mob in Brixton was all ready to cause trouble that night if you'd kept Groce in custody. Your delicate decision avoided another Brixton riot."

For a long time the Kilmuir Rules, maintained by Lord Hailsham during his long period as Lord Chancellor – rules which successfully prevented any Judge or Magistrate apart from Judge James Pickles and Lord Hailsham himself from talking to the media – (but rules which seem to have been relaxed now under the more benevolent regimes of Lords Havers and MacKay) also created a communication barrier between the Judiciary and the general public.

I first thought of writing a book about my magisterial experiences while I was at Thames and approached the Chief Magistrate, to seek his advice on the subject. Sir Frank Milton's letter in reply read:

> "The way in which this sort of enterprise is regarded in high places seems to vary with the length of the Lord Chancellor's foot . . . Kilmuir would have vetoed anything of this sort without hesitation, but I think that the present Lord Chancellor would be very broad-minded . . . I am very optimistic about your doing this." The current

Lord Chancellor was Lord Elwyn-Jones.

But, alas, I did not get round to doing it then, and Hailsham became Lord Chancellor . . . While I was at Thames the *Daily Telegraph* magazine did, with Frank's blessing, an article about me and our work in a series called "Profile of the Professions", which Frank described as having been "very good for our image". But when in 1986 the *Evening Standard* wanted to do a similar feature and I applied for permission, the representative of the Lord Chancellor's office said that Lord Hailsham did not approve of what the *Telegraph* had written and that the proposed article in the *Standard* could be published only subject to severe restrictions. The reporter, Janice Morley, then withdrew from the project, saying: "We feel the constraints we must comply with would negate a worthwhile feature. What, I wonder, would I be allowed to write?" Very little, I fear, under Kilmuir or Hailsham. Yet the essence of a good Judge or Magistrate is, in my opinion, to communicate, to explain what he or she is doing; to say, for example, on occasions why a deterrent sentence is necessary. The strict application of the Kilmuir Rules for so long restricted the extent of such communication from the Bench to a very limited section of the public: defendants. Of course some defendants become very well known to the Courts ("Good morning, Mr Crowther, and how are you today? Hope you didn't get out of bed the wrong side this morning.") At Marylebone there was for years a lady called Rosie without whose presence in the dock the day never seemed complete. The jailors used to run a book on her; not on whether she would manage a hundred appearances before the Court prior to the end of the year – that was a dead cert. – but during which month she would achieve her century. (It was usually August or September.) Such defendants one gets to know well.

But there are others on whom the Magistrate makes an indelible impression but whom he afterwards forgets. One such sent me frequent hostile missives for years, giving his name and full address (just around the corner from Horseferry Road) and I do not know what I had done to deserve such contumely.

Here is one example:

> "Dear Mr Crowther,
>
> "I object to your continued involvement in my oppression. One is a little shocked by your use of Fascist and post-Fascist methods, though one had thought you had taken the point by now and learned how to implement it . . . I am tired of your familiarity, your contempt for law and decency, your refusal of reason and your continued bitchy demands for law and justice to which you have no right.
>
> "I resent your voyeurism in my life.
>
> "Yours sincerely . . ."

I do not count this correspondent among my fans. On the other hand, when he went on his annual holiday, he would send me mildly indecent picture postcards (if I say that one of them bore the caption "Cheeky", the reader will deduce the general flavour) with quite friendly, cheerful messages. The sea air did him good.

Another correspondent wrote me only one letter. It began: "I wish to condemn you for your essential dissention and maladroit countermanding in the interest of social harmony."

Most of the rest of this lengthy epistle comprised an attack on the late Earl Mountbatten (I think because he had had some foreign blood in his veins, for the writer declared that he himself was "possessed of two beautiful blonde-haired, blue-eyed daughters and (was) suffering the recurring nightmare prospect of the alien biological anarchist for a future son-in-law"). He seemed to find some points of similarity between me and the "contemptible" Mountbatten, a comparison that I am bound to say I found flattering.

The writer concluded:

> "As documentation fodder I never fail to rise to the vocal irrelevance of administrative grist personified by the Senior Magistrate at Horseferry Road.
>
> "Deferentially, unhumbled, sans title and wealth, with right

arm raised but not forelock tugging,
Yours . . . ."

The gentleman of the postcards always took his holidays in this country, whereas a regular East End prostitute could afford an annual trip to Spain. I think that after Ronnie Bartle succeeded me at Thames he was a little shocked when a postcard signed by this lady arrived at the Court addressed to me and saying: "Having a wonderful time. Lots of sun, booze and sex. Wish you were here. You'd enjoy it. Love . . ."

She was one of my admirers, and indeed a fan of Thames Court. Here is an extract from a letter that she wrote to Matron, just to "keep in touch", after a fairly long absence from the Court because:

> "I do not drink as much now, not like I did before when I was living with that Maltese.
>
> "Oh, by the way I sent Eric Crowther a Valentine Card in the shape of a heart. You can imagine what I put inside. It is a very nice verse I made up myself. I think he is an adorable person, don't you? Well, I haven't seen him now for over five months.
>
> "Please convey my heartiest wishes to all the boys in blue at Arbour Square. They're not such a bad bunch of lads.
>
> "My love and many thanks for kind gestures I received from you and the boys in blue at Arbour Square during my short intervals there.
>
> "Really must close now, and do a pile of ironing, and then must prepare for lunch.
>
> "I remain,
>
> "Your truly grateful friend . . ."

We do have some satisfied customers, and her attitude was preferable to that of another lady of her profession who wrote to me: "Come round any time for hand relief or 'the real thing', sweetie, Love Hetty."

I think that the most amusing letter that I received at Court came from a place called Neutral Bay in Australia. Ian Botham had been summoned for assaulting a hotel porter who, it was said, had not called a taxi quickly enough to satisfy the impatient cricketer, and the case was listed for hearing at Horseferry Road on a date in May 1989. Counsel appeared on behalf of Botham to apply to break the fixture until after the middle of September as Botham had been selected to play in test matches throughout the summer. (In fact the case was never heard because the hotel porter subsequently withdrew the summons.) Such delay seemed to me at the time wholly unreasonable and unfair to the complainant and I refused the application, saying that the date the Court had fixed must stand – but I did not realize what a significant day it was until I received this letter:

"Dear Sir

"May I say how grateful we are in Australia that you have summoned Ian Botham to appear on the first day of the first Test Match against the touring Australian team.

"He is probably one of the all time great players and his absence – could you gaol him for the remainder of the summer? – will surely swing the game in the Tourists' favour.

"There's nothing sweeter than to thrash the Poms on their own soil in any game, but cricket is the sweetest and, without Beefy Botham, you have made it that much easier.

"G'Day to ya,
R. O'Connor"

But the correspondent who surprised me most was David Barnett, M.A. He seemed to hate everyone connected with the law except me, Judge Derek Clarkson and Jane Doughty. Now Clarkson is a nice, easy-going fellow, and I could understand his affection for Jane Doughty, for she was a most beautiful and competent young solicitor to whom he always referred as Doughty, L.J., which he explained as "Lovely Jane Doughty." (At her farewell party in the summer of 1989 she assured me that her decision to emigrate to Hong Kong was in no way influenced by

David Barnett's persistent attention.) Neither Judge Clarkson nor I can remember Mr Barnett at all, so for years we have both been amazed by the weekly (more frequent sometimes) verbose outpourings of his soul which have reached our homes, mine sometimes being brought personally to my flat at Lincolns Inn (although I never met him on the stairs while he was making any of these personal deliverances).

David Barnett is not an admirer of Lord Lane, the present Lord Chief Justice (but I am), or of Lord Justice Tasker Watkins (no comment) or of most other members of the higher Judiciary, and even I disappointed him once, for in September 1989 (the date comes from the post-mark on the envelope; he himself headed his letter "Year Zero") he complained to Judge Clarkson:

> "I still can't believe that Eric Crowther, O.B.E., who is a high-up in the British Council and into student welfare could stand by idly whilst I go down the tube . . . since I'm not a serious contender, meaning that I have a snowball in Hell's chance of being 'introduced' to the Honourable Society of one of the Inns of Court! As a compensation, I have rationalized: 'Anyway, I'm an historian! I only found out yesterday that the old authors, Fieta, Glanvil etc. are in the Seldon Society series, so I can have a good time in the Guildhall Library for a 'lost' year in which I hope to sort out my D.S.S. benefits and try again next term!
>
> "'Though the necessity be real, its relief is only suppositious which Hale thought oftimes the case" (Emlyn's note).
>
> "Jeremy Corbyn M.P. is a shithead swot, I say."

(I can only imagine that Mr Corbyn, like me, had failed to take up his case against the Department of Social Security.)

Realizing that Jane Doughty was engaged in pursuing Mr Barnett's oft-referred to claim against that Department, and having become very weary of his missives, I asked Jane to write to him threatening proceedings for an injunction unless he ceased molesting me. This did not have the desired effect. Not only did his epistolary efforts double, but

I started receiving from him great parcels or hampers containing books, museum catalogues, brochures and bottles of whisky and boxes of chocolates, these last two items emanating from Harrods, with whom I was having my much publicized dispute at the time. I wonder how Mr Barnett got them. Perhaps by credit card . . . ?

But when I retired David Barnett felt that the occasion was worthy of a voyage into verse, and he sent to me the following piece of doggeral, which even I think indulges in hyperbole:

"Eric Crowther Oh Bee Ee
A finer Stipe there could not be
Having the Police Court served so well
Let a 'con' bid thee a fond farewell.

"With you gone, in my Soul I think
That my Heavenborn List doth shrink
And though only of your Fame I know
Sir, I'm right damned sad to see you go.

"Oh, if only in a line or two
Of poem I could to thee get through
To tell you how terribly I you admire
And wish you all the best as you retire"

Unfortunately Mr Barnett's capacity for exaggeration exceeds his skill in scansion.

Judges in the Crown Court do not get on such intimate terms with their clients as do Stipendiary Magistrates, so Judge Clarkson should feel somewhat privileged to have established such a close relationship with David Barnett. I have sat for 20 years for at least a month a year as a Deputy Circuit Judge or as a Recorder, but only one defendant who has appeared before me in the higher Court has ever corresponded with me. This was the "Reverend" William Lynn-Walls, the greatest "con-man" I ever came across. He appeared before me and a jury at the Inner London Crown Court charged with six offences of obtaining credit by fraud from

Gamages, a worthy London store which was to close soon after the "holy man's" series of visits. (In fact he appeared at Court long after his offences because he had jumped bail in order to go and preach in Ulster for another "man of the cloth" – not in my view a great deal more commendable than Lynn-Walls, albeit for other reasons – the Reverend Ian Paisley.)

Gamages was staffed in the main by rather sweet and susceptible old ladies. Lynn-Walls, attired in clerical garb, descended upon the store six times pretending to be a bishop and obtained on credit valuable electrical goods for "the dear boys in my diocese; they do so love these discos you know, and it brings them into the fold." The items were quickly sold to satisfy his gambling addiction.

In Court he wore the cope and mitre of a bishop of the Anglican faith. During the trial the very able prosecutor asked, in the absence of the jury, my leave to cross-examine the defendant concerning his 15 previous convictions for fraud, on the ground that by wearing a bishop's robe the defendant was "putting his character in issue". I declined this request, saying that in this country anybody was free to dress as he liked – but in reality I had come to the conclusion that were Lynn-Walls given enough rope he would hang himself. I did not, however, object when the prosecutor asked Lynn-Walls if there were any proof that he had ever been consecrated a bishop.

"Yes," he replied proudly, "my barrister has the book in which my consecration is recorded" and – rather reluctantly, I thought – Ivan Lawrence, Q.C., M.P., produced a treatise entitled *Bishops at Large* by one Peter Anson, which did indeed refer to the defendant's consecration, in Ireland. I pondered over the treatise for a few minutes before remarking to Ivan: "You may think it would be better if the jury did not see this book," and he wisely agreed; for, a few pages later on, it stated that, nine days after his "consecration", the defendant had been "excommunicated" when it was discovered that the "consecration" had been conducted by a brewery worker who had complained bitterly when, following the ceremony, Lynn-Walls had stolen items from the "consecrator's" bungalow.

One Press report of the proceedings described Lynn-Walls as "impertinent to prosecuting counsel and obsequious to the Judge". Certainly every night during the long trial, as I rose, Lynn-Walls would also get up from the dock in his bishop's regalia and, crossing himself, would utter the words: "May God bless you and keep you in peace this night, my Lord." I suppose that I should have been thankful for this, because when prosecuting counsel announced that he would not be calling a police officer to give evidence against the defendant because this witness had recently been killed in a road accident, Lynn-Walls raised his arms in the air and, addressing the jury declared: "That was the hand of God."

After the long trial the jury took only 10 minutes to convict the defendant on all six counts. A few weeks later I chanced to meet one of the jurymen at a party. "You didn't take long to convict the bogus bishop," I observed. "No," he replied, "We were all agreed as soon as we went out but one of our number said: 'His counsel tried hard, so let's have a cigarette before we go back' – and we did!"

Fifteen previous convictions were then read out and his "antecedents" were described by the officer in the case, who I do not think cared for him very much. "We know him as an active fraudsman and a malicious informant. Masquerading as a clergyman, he has conducted an illegal marriage and several burial services."

I was not very kind either to Lynn-Walls. Describing him as the greatest hypocrite since Tartuffe I gave him five years, the longest sentence that I have ever given anyone except two years ago, when I had to deal with an even more despicable drug importer.

But that was not the end of the affair. During his sentence I was to receive a letter from the "Reverend" Lynn-Walls saying that his case would shortly be reviewed for parole and, as he understood that I was a personal friend of the Minister of State at the Home Office, and, as I had been very considerate to him during the trial(!), he would be grateful if I would support his application for parole if, as he anticipated, I were to be consulted.

I was indeed a personal friend of Shirley Summerskill. How Lynn-

Walls discovered this I have no idea. Shirley had married one of my friends of my student days, John Ryman, another Labour M.P. Shirley was an ardent feminist and, at the wedding, a reporter had asked her: "How will you call yourself from now on, Mrs Ryman?"

"I shall continue to be called Shirley Summerskill," she responded. "And I shall continue to call myself John Ryman," chirped in my friend. The marriage did not last long . . .

But Shirley did write to me saying that Lynn-Walls had applied for parole indicating that I would support his application, and I replied stating that I neither supported it nor opposed it. He did not get parole.

He wrote to me again from prison. He had started a training course as a plumber and painter and decorator, he said, as he was determined to abandon fraud as a means of livelihood and to make an honest contribution to society as soon as he was released; he would never don clerical garb again. I wrote back saying that I was very pleased.

He had not been long at liberty when I received another letter from him. On his release, he told me he had been given a grant by the Home Office to buy the tools of his trade, but within a few days all these had been stolen by some dreadful, dishonest person. (He seemed surprised that there was such evil in the world.) He was desperately determined to lead a decent life, but how could he do this without being able to practise the only real honest skill that he had learned? If I, who had been so sympathetic in Court, would lend him £25 (that would be worth £250 now) he would repay me at the end of the month because he had a good job lined up, if only he had the tools.

I pondered this proposition for a couple of days. If by any chance it were all genuine, it would be a tragedy if Lynn-Walls were unable to start an honest life just for the lack of a set of tools. I do not subscribe to the proverb that "the leopard never changes his spots" (and I think that I like leopards, anyway). If, on the other hand, this were just another confidence trick, I would never be troubled by Lynn-Walls again, so it would be almost worth it.

I sent him the £25 (on loan). I have never heard from him since. But I have heard of him again. His next sentence was seven years for fraud.

He did not ask to have my £25 taken into consideration . . .

Having told at some length a story out of which I did not come very well I shall now seek to redress the balance by telling what I regard as two tales of triumph. (Well, the first certainly is, anyway.)

The French have a saying for it: *"avoir l'esprit de l'escalier"*, to reflect the idea of the riposte that you would have made, if you had only thought of it at the time, and not a couple of minutes later. How many of us have not had that experience! This time I managed to give the right reply before I reached the staircase.

On a Saturday morning at West London Court four Polish people appeared before me – a mother, father, and their son aged 18 and their daughter (17) charged with (i) parking their car on a double yellow line and (ii) importing into the United Kingdom a monkey contrary to the Rabies Regulations. The second offence is regarded with great seriousness because many people in this country seem to believe that the Continent of Europe is populated not only by Brussels bureaucrats but also by rabid cats and dogs, the latter being a fear not shared by the majority of Europeans when one visits their homes and fondles their pets (although a fox suffering from rabies has recently been discovered at Rouen).

On a Friday evening the family, none of whom spoke any English – we were lucky enough to have the services of a good Polish interpreter the following day – parked their car on their first day ever in Britain outside Barkers at the height of the rush-hour (around 5 p.m.) on a double yellow line, while they went inside to look at the wonders of the English commercial scene. It contributed, of course, to an awful traffic jam and the police, armed with as many car keys as are carried by a competent car thief, proceeded to take the vehicle triumphantly to the nearest pound. As they did so the driver, a police sergeant, must have been surprised when a monkey jumped on to his shoulder. In due course all the family were arrested and kept in custody overnight. Such a serious view was taken of the matter that all four of them (including the children) were charged with both offences, and such was their ignorance of English law that all four, unrepresented in those days before there were duty solicitors, pleaded guilty to both charges.

The monkey, a pet which they had acquired while the father was working in Zaire, was not rabid. The father was able to produce certificates from two veterinary surgeons – one African, one British – giving the animal a clean bill of health. But that did not prevent our horrified authorities from destroying the poor creature during the 18 hours before the case came before the Court. There are (or were at that time) no anti-rabies notices in Polish at British ports of entry, and none of the family spoke a word of English. This, combined with their leaving the monkey in the car on a double yellow line in the middle of the rush-hour, convinced me that none of them, unfamiliar as they were with the British scene, had had the faintest idea that they were doing anything wrong. After their visit to Barkers and the car pound they had very little money left, so I said: "You have all suffered quite enough, and the children far too much. I am very sorry that on your first day in Britain it was thought necessary to keep you all in custody overnight. You will all be discharged absolutely."

There cannot have been any football matches that Saturday because the account of the monkey in the car was the lead story that afternoon in the *Evening Standard*, which gave it full (and accurate) coverage.

I was at home having dinner that evening when the telephone rang. I am one of the very few members of the Judiciary who is not ex-directory, but when Lord Denning was Master of the Rolls he lived in Lincoln's Inn and had his telephone number in the book, and what is good for Lord Denning is good for me.

The voice at the other end of the line was female and somewhat abrasive.

"You Mr Crowther?" it demanded.

"Yes," I replied.

"The Magistrate?"

"Yes," I answered, rather more apprehensively.

"Then I hope you get rabies!"

Before she could ring off I stopped her with:

"Madam!"

"Yes?" she enquired.

"Have you seen your doctor lately?"

"No. Why?"

"Because I think you've got it," and I replaced the receiver.

Near to Horseferry Road Court there is a street market called Strutton Ground where one can get some quite good bargains, so, not long after I retired, I decided to do some of my Christmas shopping there, and, whilst so engaged, I saw on a stall something that I wanted to buy for myself: six pairs of socks for the price of £3.99. I handed over a £5 note to the rather burly, red-faced trader and he started to shout at me in a manner that soon attracted a crowd.

"No, they're free to you, sir. I won't take a penny from you."

"Why ever not?"

"Because you changed my life. Listen, ladies and gentlemen. You are in the presence of a very great man, the man who changed me from a petty crook to an honest trader. For years I was selling fake perfume outside Harrods and the Courts always fined me. Sometime it was piss we put in the bottles if we couldn't find anything better, but the foreign tourists still bought it. The fines meant nothing because we were making thousands. My wife kept telling me to stop. She said it wasn't decent, but I took no notice. Then I came before Mr Crowther, the Magistrate over there" (he pointed towards the Court) "and he gave me 14 days. That gave me time to think. Now I'm an honest trader, ladies and gentlemen, as you can see, and I'm very happy, and it's all due to that gentleman there. That's why he don't have to pay for his socks."

My embarrassment was compounded when a woman standing next to me asked: "You know Judge Miskin?"

"The Recorder of London," I said. "Yes, I was having dinner with him last night."

"Lovely man. He was going to give my husband five years for robbery but then our brief called me and Judge Miskin put him on probation because we'd just got back together and he said I was a good influence. I'm Mrs Riley. Give him my love if you see him again."

Sometimes I think that our "clients" understand better what we are trying to do than the "experts" of the media.

Not always, though. Donald Hamilton has a somewhat unusual life-style. A quiet, well-spoken middle-aged Scot, he spends most of his life in prison (often having been sent there by me) with occasional visits to luxurious restaurants for sumptuous meals, because whilst in prison Donald is always planning where to go for his next gourmet dinner. He favours the West London area, but, for reasons which will become apparent, his choice of venues is becoming progressively more limited.

On the evening of his release from prison, usually after serving sentences of three months, he makes his way to a superior establishment where he is unknown, has a four-course meal assisted in its passage by two bottles of the best Burgundy, then orders a double Remy-Martin and a cigar and, when the smiling waiter presents the bill – usually between £40 and £50 – Donald says: "I have no intention of paying; call the police." Next day I, or one of my colleagues, will send him back to prison for three months.

There was one exception to this when Donald tried an Indian restaurant and the proprietor disturbed Donald's routine by refusing to call the police ("I don't want police in my establishment") and Donald was so incensed that he hit the restaurateur in the eye. That time I gave him six months.

Now we are always under pressure from the Home Office, the Howard League, N.A.C.R.O. "Liberty" and other well-meaning people not to send defendants to prison unless they are violent offenders or drug-pushers or a serious menace to society. "It does no good," they tell us. "It doesn't cure them," Certainly it had not cured Donald Hamilton, and I got to thinking if there might be any more useful and humane way of dealing with him. Three months in those days equalled two months (with remission) – it equals six weeks now, due to recent Home Office intervention – so I was able to work out exactly when I could expect to see Donald again, and it so happened that there was a very pleasant and sensible probation officer on duty that day, so I asked to see her just before the Court sat.

"Donald Hamilton is due up today," I predicted, "and I'm thinking of putting him on probation."

"Good Lord!" she exclaimed.

"Don't worry," I comforted her. "I only want a very brief report recommending probation on the ground that it hasn't been tried for years, but he'll have to remain in custody while you prepare the report, because he hasn't had a fixed address other than Pentonville for the last 15 years. But I would be very grateful if you would be available in three weeks, as I have a bright idea for disposing of Mr Hamilton, I hope once and for all." The probation officer looked apprehensive.

Three weeks later Donald Hamilton was back in the list and I sought to put my scheme into effect. First, I sent a message to the jailor that he was to be brought up at five to one; this would present no problem, as our lists were so long at West London that the morning work invariably spilled over into the afternoon. Then I asked the probation officer to come to see me with her report, a brief one in which she recommended that Mr Hamilton should be placed on probation for a short period, preferably not exceeding six months.

"Good," I told her, "I will follow the recommendation in your report, and then I want you to see Mr Hamilton and tell him that he has been extremely lucky, and you want to celebrate his good fortune with him by taking him out to lunch." (She blanched noticeably)

"Don't worry," I went on. "I want you to bring him to the nice Italian restaurant round the corner. I shall be there and I want you both to join us. I will pay the bill" (she appeared relieved). "I wonder if he's ever seen anyone pay a bill before. It could be an education for him. And I think he's an interesting man. I want to have a chat with him and find out what makes him tick."

The plan worked indeed like clockwork. Donald Hamilton was brought up at 12.55 and by one o'clock he had consented to being placed on probation for six months. Ten minutes later I was seated at a table in Café Avellino pretending to read the *Times Law Report* when the two of them, Donald Hamilton and his new-found probation officer, walked in, both beaming. I put down my paper and smiled at Mr Hamilton as I beckoned them to join me at my table.

With recognition Mr Hamilton's expression changed to one of horror. "Christ Almighty!" he cried out, "there's Mr Crowther. I'm not eating in a dump like this" – and he strode off on his own to have a meal elsewhere in circumstances which resulted next day in my providing him with free board and lodging for the next six months.

Chapter 11

Man's (or Woman's) Ingratitude

English friends often ask me: "In all your experience of working with overseas students, haven't you been disappointed, let down, found them unreliable?" The answer is – not often. They have given me much more happiness than sorrow. But one incident disturbed me very much, and still dismays me when I think of it.

The Council of Legal Education organizes lectures at the beginning of each academic year for the new intake of students to tell them about aspects of their proposed profession not covered by their formal, regular lectures. There are usually over a thousand such students. Among others, Mr Justice Megarry always lectured on "Life at the Bar" and I dealt with "The Early Years". There was a tradition that the lecturers should not receive any fees for these talks, which I always regarded as very important in formulating the attitudes of new students to their chosen career, as did also Sir Robert Megarry.

On Thursday, September 30th, 1982 I gave the talk that I had given many times before on these occasions, as also at Cumberland Lodge to students of Lincoln's Inn. I always like to illustrate my precepts by anecdotes. In support of the advice that the barrister should read his brief before going into Court I recite the story of a barrister who clearly had not done this when he appeared before me. He called a general practitioner to support his case of assault upon his client and his first question to this witness was:

"Are you Doctor Singh Mbbs?"

"No, no," replied the medical man: "I am Dr Singh. M.B.B.S. is my qualification."

To back up the proposition that one should never ask too many questions I quote the case of *Allah Bux* v. *Choudhury* which I had lost by committing just that cardinal error. The Pakistani defendant scored off me most triumphantly. (See *Advocacy for the Advocate*, second edition, pp. 100–102

Finally I urged the students to be careful of their diction.

"Speak clearly, if you speak at all; Carve every word before you let it fall" was the advice, which I quoted, of the American poet Lowell, and to illustrate what terrible confusion can arise from mispronunciation I recited the case of *Sunday* v. *Okabime* which I tried one Saturday afternoon at West London Court.

Mr Sunday, from Ghana, brought proceedings against Mr Okabime, from neighbouring Nigeria, under the Rent Act 1956 for harassment. Mr Sunday had a Pakistani barrister representing him and Mr Okabime an Indian one. There came a point in the proceedings when the Indian barrister was cross-examining Mr Sunday, and the point of the questioning appeared to be that if Mr Sunday had been harassed, he thoroughly deserved it. The cross-examination went like this:

Q: "Do you like jo'sticks, Mr Sunday?"
A: "Course I like jo'sticks. Everybody like jo'sticks."
Q: "So you like jo'sticks?"
A: "I just told you I like jo'sticks. And I like peas, too."
Q: "So you like peas as well as jo'sticks?"
A: "How many times do I have to tell you? I like peas and I like jo'sticks."
Q: "But Mr Sunday, do not the peas smell?"
A: "Why should the peas smell?"
Q: "Well, after all, Mr Sunday, the jo'sticks smell, and if the jo'sticks
smell, why should not the peas smell?"

At this point the unhappy Mr Sunday turned to me, and addressing me in a form to which I was not entitled, said desperately:

"My Lord, I don't know what he's talking about. All I want is peace and justice."

At that point I affected to have a fit of coughing and left the Bench, only returning when my laughter had become controllable.

I am quite a good mimic and in those three stories I gave the Indian (or Pakistani) questions and answers in the appropriate accent, and the Ghanaian's evidence in an African voice, just as I had done with Cockney, Irish and Scottish accents when telling stories of witnesses with those ethnic origins. In the hundred Student Cabarets that I produced for the British Council I frequently performed sketches in a turban with an Indian accent without the slightest objection from any of the thousands of Indian students who saw the shows. The only such protest that I ever had was from an Irish student who said: "Your story about the Irish implied that we are a violent people, which is quite untrue. If you ever say anything like that again up there on stage, I'll punch your big nose in."

After I had finished recounting the case of *Sunday* v. *Okabime* exactly as I have just recited it, I concluded my address with the words: "Ladies and gentlemen, I wish all of you every success and happiness in your career at the Bar."

Following the customary applause an Indian girl rose up from the middle of the left-hand side of the Old Hall in Lincoln's Inn and commented:

"I just want to say that your talk was the most grossly offensive and racialist to which I have ever been subjected, and you are quite unfit to be a lecturer or a magistrate." This remark was greeted with some applause, mainly from the area around my attacker.

I was "stunned". I could only manage to mouth the question: "Why?"

"Because," she explained, "you have told three stories about Indian people in all of which you have shown them as stupid and put them in a bad light."

At that point an English girl got up and said: "I entirely support my Indian friend. Your remarks show that you are not only racist but anti-feminist as well." A trickle of applause from the centre left followed this criticism also.

This last remark amazed me, for I have always liked and admired women. I can only think that it derived from the advice that I gave concerning closing addresses in Court: "A speech should be like a lady's dress: short enough to be interesting, but long enough to cover the subject-matter."

Then a Chinese student from Hong Kong rose to his feet: "Many of us," he said, "deplore the unjustified attack just made on the speaker, who has given us a very interesting and balanced address."

An African girl got up next: "I support the last speaker," she proclaimed. "It was a good speech."

By now I was beginning to recover sufficiently to regain control of the situation.

"I wonder if the first speaker would have made her comments if she had realized that yesterday I returned from Trinidad and Tobago where my wife and I have for the last two and a half weeks been guests in the home of a very good friend of mine, an African Judge; and that tomorrow we shall fly to India where we shall be guests of Indian friends, some of whom I have known since my student days, here in this Hall. I wonder if she realizes that those who give these preliminary lectures do so without fee, but in my case it has cost me quite a lot, as my wife and I could have flown straight from Trinidad to Bombay, but I have chosen to break my journey specially to come here to talk to you, because I like to think that these preliminary talks are of particular value to new students, especially those from overseas. If the lady had been listening to what I said she would have realized that in the first case it was the English barrister who was stupid, for not reading his brief, and in the second it was I who was stupid, for asking one question too many. In both cases Indian intelligence triumphed over English incompetence. The last case just demonstrated a complete breakdown of communication, which is to be avoided at all costs."

This statement was greeted with loud and prolonged applause from all parts of the Hall except left of centre. This encouraged me to ask: "I wonder if in the circumstances the young lady would care to withdraw her remarks?"

She rose for the last time: "No, I would not. You are a racist and I don't apologise to such people," she said, as she left the Hall.

It was the only time in my experience that hundreds of my audience had gathered round to shake my hand after a lecture. Earlier I recalled my reaction to the Indian girl's remarks as being "stunned", and I put the word in inverted commas because a Malaysian boy said to me afterwards: "You were stunned, weren't you? We could all see it. It was all so unfair."

The measure of support and encouragement that I got from the majority of students present made me believe that it was the end of the affair, but it was not. For my part, I could not forget about it, and I kept wondering if I had perhaps been wrong. More than three weeks later, on the day of our return from India, I wrote in my diary: "I have found this whole incident very disturbing and the memory of it has remained with me throughout our visit to this fascinating land, somewhat spoiling the journey for me."

The Indian girl had not forgotten about it either. Among my mail on my return home was a letter from Charles Morrison, then Dean of the Council of Legal Education, enclosing an (anonymous) article in a new publication called *Bar News*, which condemned me as racist and quite unfit to be either a Metropolitan Magistrate or a lecturer at the Council of Legal Education. It stated that my "cheap" address, aimed at making fun of ethnic minorities "could go down well as a National Front after-dinner speech."

The Dean went on to say: "Everyone who knows you and of your work for overseas students here and in the British Council for the last quarter of a century knows it is utter nonsense, of course. Nevertheless I am disturbed that you did not report the matter to me, and the members of the Council would welcome receipt of your version of the matter."

The reason why I had not reported the incident to the Dean was that less than 12 hours after it happened we were on an Indian Airlines flight to Bombay. In the next edition of *Bar News* two letters expressing a contrary opinion were published. I will abbreviate a rather lengthy one from Surindra Popat, a former pupil of mine, for whose ability I have a lot of admiration, since he has often appeared before me as an advocate:

> "I am of Indian extraction, having been born in Tanzania. I came to England in 1963 to read law and met Eric Crowther then when I started attending his lectures at the Council of Legal Education on Advocacy. I have known him very well since then.
>
> "During the time that Eric Crowther was at the Bar I did my pupillage with him in an excellent set of criminal chambers. Throughout the time I was his pupil he took a great deal of interest in me as he did in all his other pupils and in spite of being a very busy junior he always found time to teach his pupils. He often stayed up in Chambers until quite late in the evening, after conferences, to discuss his cases and to teach me the principles of advocacy and ethics at the Bar. May I add that many of his other pupils were Indians or Africans and some have gone on to high appointments in their native countries, e.g. Chief Justice Mohammed Bello of Nigeria and an Indian girl who became Deputy Attorney-General of Kenya.
>
> "In 1975 I returned from the United States to practise at the English Bar after practising in New York for five years. I found it exceedingly difficult to find a seat in a good set of Chambers having been away for so long. However, Eric Crowther, with characteristic kindness and concern, exerted all possible endeavours, including personally approaching over 10 Heads of Chambers in the Temple, to get me a tenancy. He succeeded in persuading my present Head of Chambers, F. Ashe Lincoln, Q.C., to take me on as a tenant, enabling me today to practise from a respectable English set of Chambers, something one who is unsympathetic to ethnic minorities would hardly care to do.
>
> "He has helped me in so many ways, too many in fact to enumerate, by way of advice and recommendation and indeed I still turn to him whenever I need advice on professional matters.
>
> "I think I ought to enlighten the dark recesses of your correspondent's mind by pointing out the following:

1. In 1977 Eric Crowther received an O.B.E. for his services to Commonwealth students.
2. For 30 years he was honorary student counsellor to the British Council, advising Commonwealth students on their problems, including (frequently) immigration problems.
3. He has a sense of humour, which obviously your correspondent lacks.

"I cannot help wondering if someone who is prepared to make such unfounded statements (more accurately described as character assassination) about a person who has devoted much of his life to the service of Commonwealth students, and who lacks the courage to put his or her name to the cruel innuendoes in which he or she publicly indulges, has the sound judgment that is so necessary for a prospective member of the Bar.

"Yours sincerely,

Surindra Popat, LL.M."

The other came from Anura Cooray, in my opinion one of the best of my stipendiary colleagues. (I digress for a moment to say what a pity it is, in my view, that there are not more professional Judges from the ethnic minorities, for the only two who come immediately to mind, Anura and Judge Motha Singh, Q.C., are such sterling examples of the best judicial temperament, and I feel sure that there are other such people at the Bar and among solicitors.) This was Anura's letter:

"In your recent edition of *Bar News* a letter from 'Insulted', was published, concerning a lecture given by a Metropolitan Stipendiary Magistrate, to C.L.E. students, entitled, "NO MOANING AT THE BAR – THE EARLY YEARS".

"The writer, who supposedly is a member of the 'ethnic minorities', says that the anecdotes used by the Magistrate were 'cheap' and that the lecture 'could well go down as a NATIONAL FRONT after-dinner speech'. It warns your readers to 'beware the innocence of humour: it is deceiving.'

"Anyone who has dealings with the C.L.E. will instantly recognize the Magistrate thus criticized and stamped as a racialist by the anonymous writer who does not have the dignity or courage to supply a name and address even to you. It is of course Mr Eric Crowther, O.B.E., who just happens to be the only Magistrate who lectures to Bar students in his spare time, and incidentally without payment!!

"As the first member of the so-called ethnic minorities to be appointed a Metropolitan Stipendiary Magistrate, and someone who has known Mr Crowther for many years, may I be allowed to say to your readers that these allegations are ill-conceived, unjustified and could not be further from the truth? It seems to be the work of someone who is immature, and to say the least, greatly lacking in a sense of healthy humour.

"From my early days at the Bar, I have associated with Mr Crowther. I have regularly appeared in his Court. More recently, I have shared his office at West London Magistrates' Court, when I sat there as a Deputy Magistrate. He has always gone out of his way to be kind and helpful to everyone, and in particular to those who came from the Commonwealth.

"Knowing him as I do, I am sure that he will ignore the imputations made against him, but it would be wrong for me to let it pass without putting the record straight. A word of advice, if I may, to 'Insulted' – if your sense of humour is that low, you have chosen to study for the wrong profession – so think again!

"I remain,
Yours faithfully,
Anura Cooray."

The next year I decided to give my lecture to the new in-take in exactly the same form, but at the end of it I said:

"I know it can be embarrassing to complain in public of something of which you disapprove, but I propose to stay here for a few minutes, and if any of you felt hurt or upset by anything that I said, I should be grateful if you would come and discuss it privately with me."

No one came forward, and quite soon I was left alone in the Old Hall, so the content of my lecture has not been changed.

I have not seen the English girl since (nor do I particularly want to!) but the Indian girl has appeared before me as a barrister on several occasions. She has always seemed apprehensive. She has no need to be; she has become a competent and acceptable advocate. I hope that she no longer has a chip on her shoulder, for that can be so dangerous and self-destructive.

The other disappointing experience that comes to mind reached a successful conclusion much more swiftly. A beautiful if rather well-built girl from Crete came to me in my capacity as student counsellor to the British Council at the beginning of the long hot summer of 1976 and told me of her problem. She was living with an Indian family in Highgate (I hesitated before mentioning the nationality of the family concerned after what I have just recited, but they were Indian, so why should I not say so?) and things were not working out very well. The family was very kind to her, but the house was over-crowded, the children were noisy, often playing unusual musical instruments far into the night, and she could not stand the constant smell of curry. She had an important examination in architecture to take in July and wanted my help in finding somewhere quiet and peaceful where she could study. I was working at that time at West London Court and could easily cover the five miles between the Court and my home by cycle, so my little flat in Lincoln's Inn was vacant and I offered it to her for the next three months. She was delighted. I said that I would help her move one Sunday, a decision which I regretted. My only car at that time was my Fiat Cinquecento ("Fifi") and I had to return five times to the house in Highgate to collect her incredible amount of luggage, to the wide-eyed wonder of the numerous Indian children, and then to stagger with it all up the fifty-seven steps of the narrow staircase to my flat on that sweltering Sunday afternoon, passing the door of Mrs Pugh (which happened to be ajar) who was watching what I was up to now.

Soon the complaints from the neighbours started to arrive. Like most of my guests, the Cretan succeeded in flooding the flat downstairs when she had a bath, despite my explaining to her how to, avoid this, and both neighbours downstairs complained bitterly to me on the phone at my home of her noise. (I have always felt that I had rather intolerant neighbours below me until the man directly underneath attained the age of 90 and became deaf, and until a couple of years ago the present Vice-Chancellor, Sir Nicholas Browne-Wilkinson (whose late wife used to sit with me in the Juvenile Court) moved into the flat formerly occupied by Mrs Pugh. Sir Nicholas is kindness and consideration itself, and even asks me if his (very pleasant, classical) music disturbs me!)

One of the allegations of Mrs Pugh and Mr Edgar was that the girl was always shouting and screaming in the flat. This I could not understand, as I believed her to be alone, and I could never get her on the phone to discuss it: the line was always engaged.

So one evening after Court when she had been there about two weeks I decided to mount Olympus and to call on Ariadne. The weather was still terribly hot and as I reached the foot of the stairs I could hear loud shouting coming from the top. The front door was wide open and as I entered my flat she beckoned me to take a chair while she continued with a conversation that was Greek to me. It continued for over an hour and it was difficult to tell whether she loved or hated the person at the other end of the line – both in turn, I suspected. What was clear was that she did not appreciate that one could be heard a thousand miles away on the telephone without shouting; she seemed to be trying to express herself loudly enough to cover the distance to Crete without the intervention of electricity. My main concern was the size of my forthcoming telephone bill.

When eventually it all ended she announced triumphantly: "That was my boyfriend. He is coming to stay here next week."

"No, he's not," I replied. "I told you when you came here this was a flat for one person."

I was treated to a seductive Greek pout: "A woman must have a man," she declared, philosophically.

"Not in my flat, she mustn't," I ruled. "He's not coming here and you are leaving. I have had a lot of complaints about you and from what I've heard this evening they seem fully justified. I must ask you to leave within a week."

Her manner then changed, for the worse. "You're jealous," she decided, "that's why you want to get rid of me, because you know I've got a boyfriend and you can't have me for yourself." (Nothing could have been further from the truth.) "Well, I like it here and I'm not going to leave and if you try to make me I'll ruin you. I'll say you tried to rape me."

I was somewhat "stunned" on this occasion, too. I know that current thinking is all on the woman's side in rape cases (in contrast to a few years ago) but I have sometimes remembered this incident when carrying out the preliminary examination in such cases, for I had never even attempted to kiss the girl!

When the full impact of what she had said to me had sunk in, I said: "Let's go and have a drink. Then we can discuss the future, and your boyfriend coming to England." I had no idea what solution to the problem I could put forward, but I had no wish to stay a moment longer in my flat with a woman who had just accused me of attempted rape, with hostile neighbours around, prepared to put the worst possible construction on everything.

As often happened in my life, Lord Denning provided the answer, this time unwittingly, however. As we left the flat to go towards Lincoln's Inn Fields I saw the Master of the Rolls coming towards us, and I guided Ariadne's steps towards him:

"I'd like to introduce you to the President of our Court of Appeal," I said. "Lord Denning, this young lady has a serious complaint to make against me."

"A serious complaint against YOU!" exclaimed Lord Denning. "Is this some sort of joke? What's all this about young lady?"

"Nothing. Nothing at all," she demurred. "It's all a little misunderstanding."

"Good, then let's go and have that drink. Would you care to join us, Tom?"

"No thank you. You know I don't drink, Eric."

So we had a drink on our own in celebration of the end of our "little misunderstanding" and the Greek goddess left the flat quietly (well, knowing her, probably not very quietly) within the next few days, and peas and jo'sticks reigned once more in Lincoln's Inn.

Chapter 12

3-3-3
The Bad, the Sad and the Mad

In *Last in the List* (p61) I quoted Sir Frank Milton as saying that deciding the issue of guilt presented no real difficulty to the good Magistrate, because of the burden and standard of proof but: "sentencing, that is the real problem".

When I started as a beak there were only five sentencing options open to a Magistrates' Court: immediate imprisonment for between five days and six months, a fine of up to £100, probation for between one and three years, a conditional discharge of similar duration, and an absolute discharge. Now there are at least 20 disposals available, and while all this variety is desirable, there is always the risk that one will overlook the most appropriate one.

In 1974, that great Judge, Lord Justice Lawton, who knew more about criminals than anyone else I have met except Charlie Richardson, spoke in a case called *Sargent* of the classical principles of sentencing as being "retribution, deterrence, prevention and rehabilitation". Magistrates can forget about prevention, an aim that can be achieved only in the higher Courts when dealing with really dangerous criminals, except of course when justices have to make their often very difficult bail decisions. A quarter of a century earlier Birkett, J., had declared that: "Punishment usually consists of a wise blending of the deterrent and the reformative, with retribution well in mind." and I think that every good Court is thinking equally of those three "classical" principles of retribution, deterrence and rehabilitation as it enters Court each day.

These three factors then fall to be applied to the three classes of persons who appear before the Court – the bad, the sad and the mad –

and in a busy London Magistrates' Court with perhaps 50 cases in the morning list one can predict that normally about a third of those defendants who plead or are found guilty will fall into each of these categories. It is the function of the good Court to discover which is which, and to treat them accordingly, for whatever some may say, there *are* bad people in the world who deserve to be punished.

One such case I remember from West London. It arose during the "Winter of Discontent" when, due to "industrial (in-)action", hospitals were having to get rid of patients not in urgent need of surgical attention. One such was a geriatric, some 79 years of age, who had been in the Charing Cross Hospital for about two years. One morning matron herself called upon the old lady. "I'm awfully sorry, my dear, but we haven't got the staff working now to keep you here any longer, so we'll be sending you home next week. We've been in touch with the local council and your flat is still available for you and a home-help will look in every day to see that you're all right."

When she had gone the middle-aged lady in the next bed, already recovered from some minor gynaecological operation, went over to her and said sympathetically: "What a shame! Just imagine the dirt and the dust in your flat after two years. I'm fit now and I'm going home tomorrow. Give me your keys and I'll go and clean up for you."

She certainly did clean up! With the aid of her husband they took everything of value from the old lady's flat, including even her radio, which means so much to someone who lives alone. In due course they were arrested, and confessed to their crime. Although each was of previous good character, I sent both of them to prison for this nasty, mean, premeditated crime: the woman for six months, the man for four. The reason for the distinction was that the project had clearly been the woman's brainchild; her husband had just been too weak to resist her blandishments that he should assist in the crime. When well-meaning bodies like the Howard League say that Courts should not be allowed to imprison for non-violent offences, other than supplying drugs, I often think of that case.

On supplying drugs for financial gain my basic rule has been immediate imprisonment even for a first offender, but I did depart from this precept once at Marlborough Street.

The defendant was another middle-aged woman, who did three humble but hard cleaning jobs to support her lazy ne'er-do-well violent husband and supplement his social security. The strain of living with him was such that she was "under the doctor", who for a long time had been prescribing amphetemines for her nerves. For many months she had been saving a small part of her hard-earned wages to go on a much-needed holiday with her friend, another cleaner; this part of her income she had to hide at home because if her husband found it, it would immediately be spent on drink and horses. The holiday was to be in Mallorca, in two weeks' time, and she was greatly looking forward to it; she had never been abroad before. On her fortnightly visit to the doctor he said: "I shall have to give you a prescription for an extra supply of your pills because you're going away in two weeks from now, and when you come back I'm off for a month, so I shall give you enough now to last for two months." She took the prescription to the chemist and when she got home she found that her husband had discovered her hidden treasure and had spent the lot in the public house and the betting shop. When she rebuked him, he beat her up. As she recovered from his attack, she realized how desperately she needed to get away from him for a while; she just had to have that holiday.

She had heard that you could sell drugs in Soho, and, quite fortuitously, she had a good supply. She sold one lot to an addict in Brewer Street for £5. The next person to whom she attempted to sell one of her packages was a plain clothes policeman. After a night in custody she appeared before me, battered and bewildered, next morning.

Under a lot of pressure from the media for consistency in sentencing, the Magistrates' Association is producing more and more "Guidelines" for particular offences. The trouble is that these so easily become tariffs: they seem safe; "it says here . . ." To the lazy, impatient Magistrate they are an easy substitute for thought and imagination. If supplying drugs for gain comes to be included in such guidelines the recommended penalty will inevitably (and quite properly) be immediate imprisonment. But this sad lady finished up on probation and with the aid of the Probation Service we managed to find a charity to pay for her holiday.

But it is the mad ones who cause the greatest anxiety, and, *faute de mieux,* occupy far too many cells in our over-crowded prisons; and I am serious when I say that probably a third of those appearing on charge lists in busy London Magistrates' Courts are suffering from some form of mental disorder for which the Courts have no remedy. "Care in the Community"? But what if the community does not care? And do the hospital staffs always care for the well-being of those patients, or do they think more of their own safety and well-being?

On a Friday morning an elderly Jewish gentleman with a considerable record for violence was made the subject of an order under the Mental Health Act by a Judge at the Old Bailey for a serious assault occasioning actual bodily harm. Unfortunately the Judge did not make a restriction order, but an order under what was then s.60 of the Act, the effect of which was that the defendant should be detained for such period of up to a year as the hospital should deem necessary. The defendant arrived at about lunch-time at Charing Cross Hospital.

That hospital at that time had a very "democratic" procedure under which everyone who would have to deal with a patient coming there from the Courts would have access to his papers. On seeing this man's record for violence the senior official of the National Union of Public Employees declared: "We're not having a man like that here. He might injure one of our staff. Either he leaves today, or all my staff will be out on strike." The hospital management took the line of least resistance and told the defendant that he had to go, at the same time directing him to the nearest office of the Department of Health and Social Security. He reached that office just after four, to see a notice up saying that it was closed until Monday. He had no money, no food, nowhere to spend the night. But he did have one thing with him which he had thought might prove useful, a large, sharp carving knife which he had picked up in the hospital "just in case". And in the early evening he entered a public lavatory and with the knife stabbed in the back a complete stranger who was just answering the call of nature, and who nearly died in consequence. Next morning when he appeared before me and this sorry tale was told, he said: "I had to have somewhere to spend the night, didn't I?"

I said that I blamed the hospital staff, and this condemnation of mine achieved a lot of publicity. They were very upset and asked me to go to make a visit, which I did, and we had what I think was a constructive discussion, as a result of which I had to concede that, in such cases, they labour under considerable difficulties, but not as great as those besetting the Courts when dealing with Michael Boorman, who will never say a word in Court, or Rosie McAlpine who every day when she is at liberty will break a window in order to get back into prison to complete her book of poems ("It's the only place where you can get peace and quiet") and often refuses to come out of her cell ("It's so comfortable here") and a host of others like them.

Of course the three categories of the bad, the sad and the mad frequently overlap in the same person, as for example with many of those men who make obscene telephone calls to women. The distinguished psychiatrist Dr Gerald Silverman believes that such people are potentially very dangerous and says that "the degree of seriousness with which these cases are taken by the Courts is absolutely ludicrous. I have complained again and again."

But Parliament has removed the sanction of imprisonment, and also compulsory treatment under the Mental Health Act, from this class of offender, substituting a maximum fine of £400, which cannot be imposed on somebody on Social Security, and is no deterrent to a very rich offender.

So Parliament, which in the last 20 years has given us a lot more possible disposals, has during the same period imposed even more restrictions on the way we do our work. I believe that if a custodial sentence is to have any deterrent effect it must be passed swiftly. When Judge Pickles imposed a sentence of six months in a Young Offender Institute upon a 19-year-old girl of previous good character for nine cases of stealing about £4,000 from her employers – a sentence since successfully appealed – he did so many months after her first appearance before him; and this is because the law requires one to have so many reports before jailing anyone under 21, and anyone of previous good character, and, especially, both. But her mother's very sensible comment was: "If he was going to send her to prison he should have done so at once, and not given her all this worry" – but he could not, if he were to obey the law.

Not long after I moved to Horseferry Road the duty probation officer came to see me in my room. He was one of the realists in the service.

"I wonder if you've seen your list today," he enquired. "I'm afraid you're in for a shock."

"Why?"

"Well, there are 147 cases in the list, but 103 are assaults and threatening behaviour resulting from the Chelsea-Millwall match on Saturday. I don't know what you think, Mr Crowther, but perhaps the public have had enough of this nonsense. Perhaps it's time to shut these hooligans away. On the other hand, they're nearly all under 21, so you can't do it without a Social Inquiry Report, but if you put about a hundred cases over for Social Inquiry Reports today it means that my colleagues and I will have no time to get on with any of the really deserving cases."

"Are you prepared to say that in open Court?" I inquired, and when he replied "Certainly" I went on: "Good, then when you have done so I shall certify that it is impracticable to obtain Social Inquiry Reports and I shall sentence without them." I think that it is a pity that Courts have to indulge in such ruses in order to give the public what they deserve – immediate relief from particularly annoying and distasteful types of offence.

In fact I have to admit that things did not work out very well that morning. The first five defendants pleaded guilty to quite serious offences and all received custodial sentences varying between three weeks and three months. But then word of what was happening got to those waiting outside and all the remainder pleaded Not Guilty, so their cases had to go over anyway!

My message to Parliament and the Home Office is: "Trust the Judges and the Magistrates." If they cannot be trusted they should not have been appointed in the first place. I recall one case where I definitely prevented a woman from going to gaol and from becoming a serious criminal by making what may have been an illegal order with the connivance of the defence solicitor.

She, too, was a middle-aged woman of previous good character (I do not know why so many of these difficult sentencing problems seem to concern people in that category!). She had for many years been happily married, her grown-up children had flown from the nest, and then suddenly her husband died of a heart attack. Devastated by this tragedy, and desperately lonely, she started to go the local public house and to drink heavily. It was while she was there that she was "befriended" by a person of great charm, much younger than she, who persuaded her that she was God's greatest gift to Mankind since the creation of Eve. It was not long before he moved in with her; and soon after that he put to her a business proposition. He "happened to have" a cheque book and a cheque card but they were in the name of a lady, so she would use them at various stores in Kensington High Street to acquire valuable goods, which he would dispose of, and then they would be able to have a wonderful honeymoon together. So infatuated was she with him, that this normally decent and honest woman was prepared to acquiesce in his scheme.

In the one day that it operated she obtained from various Kensington stores goods to the value of over £1,750 – and this was 12 years ago, so the figure must be multiplied many times to give a fair assessment today. But she eventually got caught that afternoon. The police released her on bail (she was of good character and had a fixed address) and next day she appeared before me, pleading guilty to the many charges. She was represented by Geoffrey Freeborough – the doyen of all the solicitors, the "Solicitor-General of West London". Now nearly 80, Geoffrey had many years earlier defended the most unfortunate Timothy John Evans, who was hanged for two murders that he almost certainly did not commit – he owed his conviction largely to the lying evidence of the serial murderer John Christie whom he had had the misfortune to have as his landlord; as strong an argument as I know against the reintroduction of the death penalty. I believe that Geoffrey felt so strongly about Evans' innocence that he conducted the (unsuccessful) appeal without a fee.

Anyway, Geoffrey put the facts before me very much as I have recited them, and I now had to sentence the trembling woman before me for a series of very serious offences, each of which of course involved forgery. I said to her: "This is a very grave matter and clearly there must be a prison sentence, but I am finding it very difficult to decide the appropriate duration. I want to think about this case overnight. You will be remanded in custody until tomorrow."

I expected Geoffrey to rise to protest, but he did not do so. When, next day, she emerged from a night in Holloway, I felt dismayed at the cruelty of what I had done: she seemed to have aged 10 years in those 24 hours. Geoffrey addressed me briefly again and I said: "The total sentence that I impose upon you is one of 12 months' imprisonment, but in view of your hitherto excellent character it will be suspended for the next two years. But I must warn you that if in the course of the next two years you choose to do anything like this again, so far as I am concerned it will be a minimum of eighteen months' immediate imprisonment for you." She left the Court a free woman.

It so happened that the following week I was at a legal dinner and found myself sitting next to Geoffrey Freeborough and I commented to him: "I expected you to rise in your wrath when I remanded that lady overnight in custody, because the fact that the Magistrate can't make up his mind is probably not a reason for failing to grant bail under the Bail Act. Then I thought you would have rushed off to a Judge in Chambers, but you did neither."

"No," said Geoffrey quietly. "I think an eager young counsel would have messed it all up by doing one of those things, and then you'd have given her 12 months straight and for that number of offences it would have been unappealable. But I'm a wily old solicitor, not an enthusiastic young barrister. I thought I knew what you had in mind. You wanted to give her one night in Holloway in the hope that that would put her off ever committing a crime again. Am I right?"

"You are right, Geoffrey."

"Would you like to know the sequel to the story?" I said that I would: how seldom does one really see the saga right through to the end! "Well, she came to see me the following day and she said that when she got home her lover was there with another cheque book and cheque card. 'This time we'll do the shops in Knightsbridge,' he said, 'and then we'll really get married and go on a world cruise. Do this for me, if you really love me.'

'But now I know you don't love me,' she protested. 'That Judge said I'd get 18 months if I got caught doing this again, but you don't care. I've had a night in Holloway and I'm not going back there for you or anyone. It was Hell.' He tried to argue with her but she would have none of it. 'All right,' he said. 'If you're not prepared to do things my way, I'm off.'

'Good' she said – and he left to find some other victim.

"But if you had given her 12 months suspended for two years without that night inside she would have done it again, because she was so infatuated with him."

"Yes, Geoffrey, but it was probably an illegal order"; and we both smiled, thinking that if one night in custody will sufficiently deter someone, it is surely better than 18 months' imprisonment.

All the do-gooders (who seem to want to support the do-harmers) constantly (but rather vaguely) say that we imprison more people than any other Western European country, and ask why. When I talk to defence lawyers in Spain they often ask my why the Spanish Courts imprison more defendants than any other country in the European Community and they wonder why. Certainly Italy has far more untried people languishing in gaol – sometimes for 10 years or more – and this I regard as much more serious.

What these protagonists of "Set the people free" (to commit more crimes) never seem to direct their attention to is that a lot more people are committing serious crime than was the case just over a quarter of a century ago. Thirty years ago there were 28 stipendiary Magistrates in

London; now there are over 50. In addition thousands of lay justices are adjudicating in Inner London, whereas there were none of those until the mid-1960s.

When I was at the Bar there were three Inner London Courts dealing with all serious crime: the Old Bailey with four Courtrooms, London Sessions also with four, and Middlesex Sessions with three. Now the Old Bailey has 39 Courtrooms (I think), the Inner London Crown Court 15, Middlesex Crown Court 7, and vast new complexes have been created at Southwark, Snaresbrook, Isleworth, Wood Green Harrow and Surbiton to deal with the growing menace to the ordinary citizen of serious crime.

When I started at the Bar there was a well-known saying: "He that takes what isn't his'n, if he's caught will go to prison."

This must be amended now to read:

"If he's caught he will not go to prison until conditional discharge, fine, probation, community service and the day training centre have all been tried and failed." And it is not unusual to find a defendant who has made 15 appearances before Courts before a custodial sentence has been imposed – and then, in my opinion, one that is often too long to serve a useful purpose. Something has got to be done to reduce the appalling figures for crime, so often motivated by greed, and my own proposal derives to some extent from the case of the Kensington lady with the cheque card, and to an even greater extent from my personal experience.

My first three days in the Navy were unmitigated hell. I was required to rise at the hour of 5 a.m. (a time of whose existence I had previously been unaware), proceed everywhere "at the double", salute smartly a group of gentlemen in fancy dress, eat (when I felt up to it) food matched in its foulness only by the vocabulary of most of my companions, and receive orders never delivered at less than a deafening 120 decibels. Yet my only crime, to merit such continuous torture, was to have been born more than 18 years before the end of World War Two. If, during those first three days, a kindly officer (if such a person existed) had offered me a tablet of cyanide, I would gladly have consumed it.

At the end of three days I was herded onto a lorry to another part of

England for three months of general training: lots of PT, square-bashing, enforced listening to the tediously lurid reminiscences of hard-bitten Petty Officers. Yet I began to find some interest and even merit in my companions, and to have a sense of "belonging", after all. Even so, had I had the opportunity (and the money) to buy myself out, I would have done so, eagerly.

But when, three years later, my demob-day drew nigh, the companionship of my fellows was so dear to me, and the routine of service life so familiar and unthinkingly easy, that I volunteered to stay for an extra period, and ultimately returned to civilian life with considerable misgivings and many regrets.

Many years later I had an operation. My own surgeon was very taciturn, but shortly afterwards while convalescing I chanced to meet another specialist in my complaint, to whom I enthusiastically regaled the details of my recent experience. "When," I asked, "can I return to full activity, like Scottish dancing?" "The rules are very simple," he replied. "Remember the three threes. For three days after your operation you should do absolutely nothing, for three months do very little, and after three years, if there have been no repercussions, you can forget all about it."

Of what possible interest can my Naval Service and, even more tedious, my operation, be to readers of this book? I believe that they have a relevance to a problem that is troubling every thinking person today: the appalling growth of serious crime in our country, especially among young people.

To cope with this in an entirely new way, the Children and Young Persons Act of 1969 was introduced and has been added to by the Criminal Justice Acts of 1988 and 1991. Those who drafted them had the best of motives. "Treatment" was to replace punishment; "caring" to be substituted for "scaring". Yet who that is concerned with Justice in the Juvenile Courts or is concerned about Justice at all can doubt that it has been a failure? It is no use pleading, as its protagonists still do, to give it more time. If it is given much longer we shall be in danger of breeding a generation which sees crime as the normal way of acquiring property, and which replaces order by disorder, tolerance by hooliganism.

What is to be done to stop this avalanche towards anarchy? I would like to suggest an adaptation of the "3-3-3" remedy. For his first "arrestable offence" (and it may well be that the definition of this would have to be amended to exclude some relatively minor matters such as a first offence of shoplifting involving giving way to sudden temptation – but I would not exclude possession of drugs; those youngsters who buy cannabis are unthinking supporters of General Noriega and similar gangsters.) the defendant, young or old, male or female, would undergo a custodial sentence, in an establishment appropriate to his age, of a minimum of three days; for his second, for a minimum of three months; for his third, for a minimum of three years. These sentences, with no remission on the first two, would be mandatory in the absence of "special reasons", such as diminished mental responsibility, evidence of which would have to be given on oath, and these would be construed at least as strictly as special reasons in driving cases – and I mean special reasons, not "special mitigating circumstances". There should then be no difference in sentencing between "tough" Benches and "soft" Benches. I envisage that the minimum sentence would be the normal sentence (though not necessarily so – it would obviously not be appropriate for a long-term fraudsman when at last found out, or for a first rapist) and that conditions on the first two sentences (three days and three months) should be extremely severe, following the pattern of the "short, sharp shock" originally envisaged, but long since abandoned, in the Detention Centre, or the harsh regime of the brief German Jugendarrest.

I do not believe that many would return for the second sentence of three months, and it may be that anyone who came back for this three years (for which, in view of the duration of the sentence, a less stringent regime, with the possibility of some form of corrective training and of *earned* remission, would be appropriate) would, in colloquial terms, "need his head examining" so that a report of a psychiatrist should be sought in suitable cases, to see if it affords a "special reason", in which case he should be called and questioned by the Court. Any who came back for a fourth time (and vast numbers do at the moment) would have to be treated as recidivists, with long sentences for the protection of the public, but under much milder conditions.

One objection to the "3-3-3" method is that it could lead to an employed person losing his job for a first offence. To overcome this, in these days of the five-day week, the three days would commence at a designated prison at 6 p.m. on the Friday following pronouncement of sentence (or immediately in the case of a Friday Court) and end at 6 a.m. on the following Monday. If without good reason the defendant failed to turn up as required he would automatically become eligible for Stage Two – three months. Of course this would involve more work for hard-pressed prison staff at week-ends and, for them, a further interference with what has become the English Sabbath (Saturday), and these prison officers, supplemented by part-time week-end helpers if necessary, would have to be compensated with extra pay for unsocial hours and time off in lieu during the week, but it happens in Scandinavia and if, as a result, the crime rate is cut, so would be the expense of keeping an ever-increasing number of case-hardened criminals for longer periods in custody, which is the present unsatisfactory situation. My answer to the criticism that 3-3-3 would cause more overcrowding of penal establishments at week-ends is that this is just one of the hardships that those who choose to commit crimes would have to bear in the interests of their victims and, more importantly, their potential victims.

Crime causes suffering: suffering for the victim every time and suffering for the criminal and his family when he gets caught and is punished. It is our duty to alleviate suffering of the innocent, and sometimes we have to be cruel to be kind. If the imposition of a three-day custodial sentence on a criminal, of whatever age, for his first serious offence, with the certainty that his next one would attract a loss of liberty at least 30 times as long, might reduce the suffering of all concerned, is not 3-3-3 an experiment worth trying?

If, after my first three days in the Armed Forces of the Crown, some influential person had secured my release, nothing in the world would have got me back.

Chapter 13

A Citizen of the World (if you can get through Immigration . . .)

I suppose that Sir Winston Churchill is the most loved and most admired of all our statesmen this century. Affection for him seems to transcend class and party, and rightly so when one considers what he did for this country, and for the world, half a century ago. How grievously disappointed he must have been when the nation, only three months after the war in Europe ended, turned its back on him in an election, whose result represented revolt against the "officer class", a rebellion which was supported by Jane of the *Daily Mirror*, who featured in the first British "strip" cartoon.

Hitler had declared that when his troops had subdued Britain, Churchill's body would be hung from a tree in Trafalgar Square. In this he betrayed a peculiar botanical ignorance, unless he was prepared to await the arrival of the Norwegian Christmas tree . . . But Churchill's reaction to his war-time enemies was more magnanimous. Before he was ousted from office he declared: "For nearly six years we have been engaged against the Germans in brutal and bloody conflict. But now it is over, and we must welcome Germany back into the family of Europe as our friend and our partner." His beliefs and utterances paved the way to the European Community, our entrance to which was achieved only by the vision and effort of Edward Heath (and we have had no war in Europe for 45 years now, an incredible time, historically) and Churchill once accorded to himself, boastfully but justifiably, the title of "First Citizen of the World".

I too like to think of myself, not too modestly, as a "Citizen of the

World". I was encouraged in this direction by my 30 years of work for the British Council, which has resulted in my not wanting my country to go to war with any other nation, and my ambition to visit every country on this earth. So far I have been to 60 other lands, which constitutes over a third of the member states of the United Nations.

But, as the world gets smaller, the difficulties of getting into other countries increase, as Governments of all political hues work to keep out those whose opinions or way of life seems in any way inconvenient. I will remember my first visit to the United States, which took place in the McCarthy era. After five hours of standing in line I was eventually accorded an interview with an immigration officer.

"You a Communist?" he demanded.

"No."

"Your father a Communist?"

"No."

"Your grandfather a Communist?"

"I don't think there was Communism in my grandfather's day."

"Listen, buddy, don't get fresh with me if you want to enter this country."

"Oh, sorry. It's just a different sense of humour."

He went on questioning me, mainly about my political affiliations – or rather the lack of them – for about another 15 minutes. At the end of this inquisition he returned to his main theme:

"You sure you're not a Communist."

"No. I'm not sure," I replied. "When I arrived here I was very anti-Communist, but after talking to you for the last quarter of an hour I think I have become one."

"Okay, buddy," he said severely, pulling down his cap. "I warned you before about being funny. You wanted to stay here for three weeks. I'm sending you back in three days, on the boat you came on. If it was goin' sooner, you'd be goin' sooner. We don't want people like you around." So 60 hours later I sailed back past the Statue of Liberty.

Some British immigration officers are worse than that – really! In my capacity as Student Counsellor at the British Council and subsequently as

"Honorary Officer" at International Students House I heard many heart-rending tales of insensitivity, rudeness, malice and even sadism, and so low was the success rate of my appeals that in November 1988 I gave up this kind of advice altogether: I could not stand it any more.

Before Britain joined the European Community we had a very delightful young Italian friend, and when she went home after a year of studying here we said to her: "Come and visit us any time, whenever you feel like it" – just as many warm-hearted Italians have extended the same invitation to me, although I have never had any difficulties with the Italian authorities.

Emilia duly arrived, but without warning us, for a short holiday, so that there was no answer to the telephone when the immigration officer rang – we were both at work – and she had no "letter of invitation" with her. She also had very little money. The immigration officer was prepared to jump to conclusions. "I know what you've come for. I don't believe a word about these friends of yours. We've got quite enough prostitutes of our own without having foreign ones. I'm sending you straight back to Rome" – and he did. It was many years before she could be persuaded to come to Britain again. Now this highly respectable lady is married to a prominent Italian official. I wonder what that immigration officer did for the reputation of this country.

It was after Spain joined the E.E.C., but before she had become a full member, that I met a charming Judge in Madrid who said that he would like to send his 20-year-old son over to England for a holiday, and I said that he could stay with us, and on this occasion I did supply a letter of invitation. The young man spoke quite good English and was eminently respectable. He had adequate funds to support himself for the three weeks that he was to spend in London, and showed his money and my letter to the immigration officer.

"Supposing on your first night in London you were robbed of all your money, what would you do?" this individual asked in quite a friendly way.

The Spanish boy smiled and replied: "Well, I suppose I would have to go and wash up in a restaurant."

The immigration officer's manner changed: "So you are quite prepared to break our laws about aliens not working? We don't want people like you here . . . I am sending you straight back." And he did. The young man was not even allowed to make a telephone call to me; but you can imagine what his father said when he did so.

"Trick questions" like that were commonplace until a few years ago, but I understand that, following lots of protests, the Home Office does forbid them now. But is anyone as cruel and cunning as that immigration officer suitable to hold public office? And do the citizens of this country really want to create a "Fortress Britain"? Perhaps they do. A young American friend of ours who stayed with us over a recent Christmas does not seem to hold our people in very high esteem. He remarked over dinner: "If you held referenda in the United Kingdom on the restoration of the death penalty and whether all foreigners should be kept out of Britain, there would be a substantial majority in favour of both resolutions, but a minority would say: 'Let a few foreigners in so that they can feature in public executions!'" I think that his unjustifiable bitterness towards us as a people derived entirely from his only two experiences of our immigration authorities. On the occasion of his first visit he was sent back on the ground that he did not have enough money to sustain himself without working illegally (although in my view his funds were ample) so, when he returned, he had a surplus of money and was detained in custody for 36 hours on the basis that no young person would have that amount of cash unless he were involved in drug-trafficking. He was, however, released, and given a visa for a month on Christmas Eve after vigorous and time-consuming representations by me on his behalf, and we spent a very pleasant (drug-free) festive season with him.

"Immigration cases", like drug matters, were rare when I started sitting as a Magistrate in 1968 but now in London they are an everyday occurrence. Some of the defendants are overstayers; others are students who come here on grants and then, for political reasons, arising in their own countries, find their funds cut off. Three choices are then open to them: to go home, their courses uncompleted, without a qualification; to resort to crime; or to take work, often at night, cleaning hotels – work which no English person seems to want to do. A great deal of police and immigration officers' time is deployed in tracking down the "criminals" in the third category who, when apprehended, will often be kept in custody for more than 24 hours before being brought to "justice", although the employers never seem to get prosecuted. And what represents "justice" in such cases? To me and a good many of my stipendiary colleagues it was a conditional discharge for a first offence, but some lay justices take a much more serious view, even recommending deportation (despite Lord Justice Lawton's advice in *R* v. *Nabavi* that such a drastic measure should be reserved only for "really serious cases") and ordering that the defendant should be kept indefinitely in custody for a period sometimes approaching a year while the Home Office, which constantly complains of the size of the nightly prison population, makes up its mind whether to deport or not. (My impression is that the majority of people so detained by Magistrates do eventually get deported.) I do not think that we should like it if our sons and daughters who had done a little work abroad to tide over unexpectedly hard times were detained for months in prison by a foreign power and then deported, and it does nothing to promote harmony among the nations.

The difficulty that lay justices face is that they deal with a lot fewer of these cases than stipendiaries, and, being unfamiliar with them, they look to Home Office officials, who often attend Court, for advice. This is usually adverse to the defendant.

When, in the 1970s, this class of case started to crop up in London, I was in the same position, and whenever there was an immigration case one of the men from the "A.R.D." (the Aliens Registration Department) would step forward to give advice. There were two of them, Mr Moore and Mr Jarvis, and both of them appeared respectable, decent, articulate and knowledgeable, and at first I was disposed to follow the advice that they proffered. But although they looked very much alike, after a while I found that they were very different in attitude and approach. Mr Jarvis was fair and balanced and willing, if he could, to plead matters in favour of the errant immigrant: Mr Moore never had a good word to say for any of them. His summary of the facts always put the defendant in the worst possible light (even if he were an overstayer by a mere 72 hours) and would invariably finish with the following "spiel":

"Of course his having admitted this offence it is open to Your Worship to make a recommendation for deportation in this case and I would urge you to do so because it considerably strengthens the Home Secretary's hand. If you do decide to recommend for deportation, the question then arises whether or not to detain the defendant in custody. It is of course entirely a matter for you, but may I ask you to give serious consideration to detaining the defendant in custody, as it is our experience that almost invariably the defendant who is not detained in custody will 'go to ground' and not be seen again for many months and it is difficult to see, is it not, how he can survive without resorting to crime? It is therefore very much in the public interest – and perhaps in his own – that he should be kept in custody."

I dealt with several of these cases before I realized that Mr Jarvis never gave this advice, and Mr Moore's "lock 'em up and get rid of 'em" was a policy that he was pursuing on his own in cases before me, and I very much regret that I followed his advice in a few earlier cases before I got wise to him.

We met our Waterloo at West London (if that is not a contradiction in geographical terms) in 1977. Harold Wilson's first Minister of State in charge of immigration at the Home Office was Alex Lyons, an eminently fair, kind and reasonable man (now, I believe, a Social Democrat). In the 1970s the National Front, although they never gained a Parliamentary seat, were starting to have more success in both Parliamentary and local elections – mainly at the expense of the Labour Party. Their sole political platform was of course: "Keep and get the foreigners out – especially the blacks!" Harold Wilson was nothing if not a politician and he replaced Alex Lyons by the tough (oh, so tough! – I know; she was a good personal friend) Shirley Summerskill, with, I suspect (although she never told me so) instructions to implement a much tougher immigration policy. If the Labour Party could be seen to be going some way along the National Front line on this matter, would not their defectors to that evil cause return to the fold? It was while Shirley was Minister of State in this capacity that I started to see students in tears for the first time in my "surgery". (Of course things were to get even worse when eventually David Waddington, later the Home Secretary, came to hold that office.)

And so the London Courts started to see a lot less of Mr Jarvis and a lot more of Mr Moore, who appeared before me with all the papers in the case of a 23-year-old Pole who was being prosecuted for falsely representing that he was married to a British person in order illegally to stay in the country. Imagine in those days the fate of being forced back to Poland, which was what Mr Moore was urging!

The defendant had been married two years previously in England to the lady. He produced a certificate to this effect, combined with the lady, who said that they were living together and buying their home on mortgage, and her mother, who said that the couple had been engaged for a year before their wedding and that they were an extremely happy pair.

"Well Mr Moore," I asked somewhat smugly, "what do you say to all that?"

Mr Moore smiled at me, indulgently. "A marriage of convenience, Your Worship. It's obvious."

"It's not obvious to me, Mr Moore. Explain yourself."

Mr Moore regarded me with that patient look which is normally reserved for addresses to rather backward children.

"It's obviously a marriage of convenience. They've been married for two years and there are no children – not even on the way – and she is 10 years older than he."

My patience has always been one of my few virtues, but I felt that it was beginning to desert me.

"And supposing, Mr Moore, that he had been 10 years older than she, would you have put that forward as an argument in support of a marriage of convenience?"

"Of course not!" he replied contemptuously.

"I consider your attitude absolutely disgraceful," I commented. "I shall report this matter with a view to your prosecution under the Sex

Discrimination Act" – and that night I wrote to the Home Secretary about the case.

In fairness to Mr Moore, it is right to say that his report to the Lord Chancellor next day about my conduct of the case and my rudeness to him could not have been occasioned by my complaint against him, as he would not have known about it at the time. He felt as deeply about the matter as I did.

I was seen in the Home Office by the Permanent Secretary to the Home Office, who resembled, to me, the Secretary to the Cabinet in "Yes, Prime Minister". Everything was for the best in the best of all possible worlds, and the Home Office was not responsible for anything, anyway. The Aliens Registration Department was nothing to do with the Home Office; it was a department of the Metropolitan Police.

But was not the Metropolitan Police under the Home Office? I inquired, in my innocence.

"In theory, yes, but in practice, no. The Metropolitan Police is an autonomous body with which the Home Secretary has no wish to interfere. Your complaint will have to be re-directed to the Commissioner for Metropolitan Police."

He went on to say that he was delighted that I was so pleased with the way Mr Jarvis did his work. (He seemed to be willing to accept the credit for Mr Jarvis but not the blame for Mr Moore.) In any case, although he had no control over the situation, he thought that it would be possible to ensure that Mr Moore did his work in Courts other than West London in the future.

"That means he'll be doing his harm, as I see it, in Courts which are not familiar with him and his methods, instead of with me who can cope with him," I protested.

"Ah, well," he said blandly, and rather inappropriately, "that's the luck of the draw, isn't it? I mustn't keep you longer; I'm sure you have lots of things to do. Do let my successor know if you have any more problems. I'm retiring next month, you see. Goodbye. It has been nice meeting you." I never saw him – or Mr Moore – again. But a lot more power has been given to the Mr Moores of this country by the Immigration

Act of 1988 and the 1991 Regulations. Is that something of which we as a nation should be proud?

I suppose that the reason why one of the last cases with which I dealt in my capacity as Student Counsellor, that of Herman Gelvez, made me so angry was because he was the brother of a friend of mine. I will conclude this chapter with the letter that I wrote to the Under-Secretary of State at the Home Office in February 1989 which finished with seven questions. Like my earlier letters in the case to the Home Office Immigration Department it produced no answers, but as all the questions were rhetorical I suppose it could be argued that they did not need a reply. But I think the nation ought to want the Home Office to answer for the harm that is being done in its name.

"Immigration: The Case of Herman Gelvez"

"Ruth Gelvez came to England from Colombia as an au pair in 1975. She soon became a very good friend of my wife and myself. She has lived in England most of the time since her arrival. When she married in August, 1981, my wife and I were 'witnesses' at the wedding in substitution for Ruth's parents in Colombia. Both Ruth and her husband have rights of residence and permits to work here. They are honest, hardworking people, who now have two children and are buying their own house on mortgage. Neither has ever been in trouble with the police. Since the marriage, both have been close friends of my wife (a lay Magistrate) and myself.

"Ruth has a younger brother called Herman, aged 24, who wanted to visit her and see England. He had not been abroad before. He bought a return ticket with Avianca, valid for 60 days. The plan was that he should live with Ruth and her husband during his holiday and they would look after him. He duly arrived at Heathrow, after that long flight from South America, at 7.30pm on September 20, 1988. He did not emerge to be greeted by his sister, brother-in-law and his nephew and niece, who were waiting for him.

"He was interrogated into the early hours of the morning by an immigration officer, Mr D L George, who was suspicious of Herman's motives in coming to England. Apparently the amount of money that Herman had with him (£450) was wrong; Herman is still not sure if it was too little or too much, but it was not right. At 5am on September 21, Herman was told that he would be returned to Bogata and he was transferred to Harmondsworth Detention Centre to await deportation on the next Avianca flight. He remained there until 11 o'clock that night.

"Ruth 'phoned me during the night of 20th/21st. She had seen Mr George after many hours of waiting and pleaded with him. 'He was like a stone.' I wanted to speak to him to vouch for the family's respectability and offer myself as a guarantor for Herman. Mr George refused to speak to me.

"That day I tried to get in touch with Michael Portillo, Ruth's Member of Parliament, but he was on holiday. However, a Mr Day, who was looking after Mr Portillo's affairs, put a stop on Herman's deportation with the result that at 11pm Herman was given 'Exceptional Leave to Remain' and released into the custody of his by now distraught sister. I was asked to write to Mr Portillo explaining my interest in the case and did so on September 22.

"Early in October, Marks and Spencer, for whom Ruth had previously worked as a cashier, asked Ruth to return to help them cope with the pre-Christmas rush. With both Ruth and her husband out at work all day Herman got bored. Speaking no English on arrival he found a place to study full-time in a local language school, St George's College, which from previous experience of the establishment I happen to know is an excellent school.

"He undertook a full-time course of English there and Ruth paid his fees for that term. Herman felt that a knowledge of English would be very useful to him in Colombia, and if in June he could get the cherished "Cambridge Certificate of Proficiency" he would be assured of a good job back home. So he worked hard, was punctual and regular in attendance, always handed in diligent homework on time and got excellent reports from his teachers. But he had committed the ultimate crime in the eyes of the immigration authorities: he had *changed his mind* as to the purpose of his visit.

"On October 24, I wrote to the Home Office Immigration Department in Croydon explaining fully the change in Herman's status and the reasons for it. I took great care to use all the appropriate reference numbers and to address the envelope correctly. I thought that the immigration authorities might be pleased that Herman was subscribing to private education as a full-time student. Up to now I have had no reply.

"Herman did hear, however. St George's College insisted that if Herman were to go through to the Proficiency Examination in June he should pay the fees for the Spring term by January 16 at the latest. These fees had to be 'non-returnable' because of Home Office suspicions that private English language schools are prepared to involve themselves in a conspiracy with foreign students to defeat the immigration regulations. Ruth rang me on Friday 13, an inauspicious day, to ask my advice as to whether she should pay the £304 required to secure a place for Herman until Easter. I replied, unwisely as it turned out: "No news is usually good news. Pay the fees, or the Home Office won't believe that he is a genuine student." So on January 16 Ruth parted with over £300 of hard-earned money which she could ill afford and Herman resumed his studies.

"No acknowledgment or other communication had been received from the Home Office, but Herman received a letter from the Immigration Department on Tuesday 17. It informed him that he had to report to Heathrow on Thursday 19 for deportation that day and that if he failed to do so he would be arrested and might be kept in prison. The Home Office, which had taken nearly four months to reach their decision, gave him two days to get his affairs in order.

"On hearing of this I instructed a solicitor to take action, and Bill Relton worked for 11 hours that day to try to see that Justice was done. In the result Ashe Lincoln, Q.C., appeared in the High Court on Wednesday January 18 to ask for a Judicial Review. I cannot praise too highly these two gentlemen who worked so hard for

Herman and for Ruth without financial reward, for they realized that their clients had very little money. Not all lawyers are avaricious – in fact very few are, in my experience.

"Mr Justice Schiemann was kind, courteous and concerned. But he held – rightly I think – that there was insufficient material before him for him to order a Judicial Review. By ordering Herman's departure within two days the Home Office had effectively stymied any effective application. However, the learned Judge expressed his deep concern at the precipitate action of the Home Office in ordering deportation in two days, especially as they had not had either the time or the courtesy to answer my letter in a period of nearly three months. He recommended to the lawyers that they should get in touch with the most senior official possible in the Immigration Department to indicate the High Court's displeasure at the manner in which this case had been conducted and his wish that there should be a stay of execution of the deportation order for long enough to enable proper documentation to be filed on behalf of Herman.

"So, next morning – on the day of the proposed deportation – Bill Relton got in touch with Miss Webber of Immigration at Heathrow Airport. Miss Webber was the only person apart from the lawyers to come out of this saga with credit. She was kind, considerate and reasonable. I doubt if she has much of a future in the immigration service.

"Bill told her that Herman did not wish to return to his native land at the expense of the British public. When he decided that he wished to stay on here until just after his examinations in June 1989, he had been to a travel agent who had said that, subject to seat availability, he could return by Avianca on his ticket by any flight within a year of his arrival in September 1988. Miss Webber said that his enforced departure would be delayed by a week to January 26, and if during that time he could provide proof that within a reasonable time he would be flying back at his own expense by Avianca he would not be deported. By now Herman was getting rather fed up with Britain and decided to return on his own ticket by the Avianca flight of Saturday January 28.

"A misfortune then arose for which I do not think that Herman can be blamed (although the Immigration Department took the contrary view). Avianca had cancelled its flight of Saturday January 21. All their disappointed passengers were offered the option of travelling on January 28. There was no room for Herman on that flight. He was given a seat on Tuesday January 31.

"Ruth was very worried (not without justification) that the cancellation of that Avianca flight would result in her brother finishing up in gaol and asked me to 'phone Miss Webber, who had also been kind enough to ring her and tell her not to worry. But when I tried to get through to Miss Webber it was her day off and unfortunately I got Mrs Pounj. She addressed me slowly and lengthily, in the manner normally reserved for an imbecile child, on how sinful Herman had been in changing his mind and therefore how he was to be regarded as wholly untrustworthy. The learned Judge had been completely wrong to describe the Immigration Department's action as precipitate. It had taken them nearly four months to make a decision! I suggested that if Herman were allowed to complete the part of the course for which Ruth had paid, I would guarantee personally to take him to the airport and see that he boarded the 'plane on Saturday March 18. Mrs Pounj said that this was quite unacceptable. However, she did make me a promise, subsequently to be broken, that if Herman turned up at the airport on the 26 in time for his deportation but with a valid ticket to board a plane within a reasonable time thereafter he would not be deported. So, on my advice, he attended at Heathrow on Thursday January 26 with his own ticket, revalidated for Tuesday January 31. Neither Miss Webber nor Mrs Pounj was there, but a male immigration officer, whose name Ruth did not get, refused to allow Herman to stay on for those remaining five days and, having told Ruth and Herman that if he did not board the 'plane there and then he would be arrested and might spend many months in an English prison, refused to listen to any further argument and simply stood holding his watch and announcing periodically (as in "The Man Who Came to Dinner") how many minutes Herman had left in which to board the 'plane if he were to avoid arrest for a criminal offence. Under this pressure Herman got in the 'plane and departed from England. A girl of 16 was taken weeping from her family and forced on to the same 'plane.

"In Victorian times deportation was regarded as the second most severe sanction, after capital punishment. As a Magistrate I am required to be, and I am glad to be, non-political. I therefore make no comment on the facts that I have recited, but I would like to ask the Home Secretary certain questions, without any great hope, after the fate of my letter of October 24 1988, that they will be answered:

"1. What wrong had Herman Gelvez done to deserve such condign punishment?

2. What harm would have ensued to the British public if he had been allowed to stay on until Easter or even June as a full-time student with his fees paid in that private school?

3. The Home Secretary frequently states that his immigration policy is 'firm and fair'. What impression of British fairness does the Home Secretary think that such conduct on the part of his officials is creating abroad?

4. How many visitors are subjected to this sort of treatment at ports of entry every day?

5. Was it necessary to inflict so much misery on Herman, on Ruth and on the family?

6. Would it not have been better to let Herman travel back at his own expense on January 31 than to deport him on January 26 at a cost of £722 to either British Airways (the carrier who took him from England) or the British taxpayer?

7. 'Who will ever be able to make some stubborn, narrow-minded human beings understand other people's sorrows and joys?' his is not my question, but one that Alexander Solzhenitsyn wrote

to Stalin. For asking it he got eight years' imprisonment – and was deported.
Yours sincerely"

Saint-Exupéry's idealistic Little Prince looked for a land of liberty, a universe without frontiers. He would have to take care not to land in the Britain of the 1990s as he made his journey to the stars.

Chapter 14

The Last Day

Friday September 22, 1989, was my very last day of sitting as a Magistrate. The previous night we had had my farewell party at Horseferry Road Court, and several guests suggested that Elke should bring me to the Court for my last day to ensure that I arrived in good time. I do not enjoy a particularly good reputation for punctuality, although I have actually arrived at Court late only twice in 21 years. Neither Elke nor I appreciated the significance of these injunctions for early arrival, but in the event we got there a quarter of an hour before the Court sat, which should have been just right for what the conspirators had plotted. But – "the best laid plans of mice and men . . . " and just as I entered my room John Dooley rang me on my private 'phone to say "goodbye" on my last day. John, a gentle person from Southern Ireland had, as I recited in the third chapter, been one of my regular drunks for 16 years. Following a spell in custody which I awarded him when he was really ill, he resolved to give up drink and attend meetings of Alcoholics Anonymous, and he had accepted my invitation to lunch a week earlier, when he looked smart and well and had clearly kept to his resolution. John had a lot to say about his progress, of which he had every reason to be proud, and I did not want to cut him short, so I chatted with him for at least 15 minutes, oblivious of the consternation that this delay was causing outside in the corridor. When eventually I put down the receiver there was a peremptory knock on the door and the burly and authoritative Sergeant Smith entered my room with a possé of police.

"May I ask you to come this way, sir?" invited the Sergeant, and I accompanied them downstairs, thinking that some sort of presentation was to be made to me by the police (a bottle of whiskey, perhaps?). Not a bit of it. I was unceremoniously bundled into a cell where to my horror I found myself in close proximity with one of our most vicious and violent drunks, Anthony Maxwell, glaring at me and baring his teeth like a wild enraged tiger. My ordeal was very brief – no more than a few seconds – before the door was opened and the senior jailor, "the Bishop", ordered firmly: "This way please" and led me into the dock of Court Number One, which I noticed from my unaccustomed position seemed unusually crowded.

My young colleague Roger Davies was presiding, with Mrs Joan Gray, the urbane Chairman of the lay justices, sitting beside him.

Miss Glenn, the delightful Deputy Chief Clerk, ordered me to stand. "Eric Crowther," she declared, "you arrived late and so have been convicted in your absence of a number of offences. These comprise wandering abroad and failing to give a good account of yourself, being an incorrigible rogue, wasting police time and organizing and performing Scottish Dancing without a music and dancing licence. The Duty Solicitor has been appointed to mitigate on your behalf, if there is any mitigation." I felt tempted to say that my licence was at Swansea (an excuse frequently proffered by errant motorists) but decided to let Arnold Stevenson, the doyen of the local solicitor advocates, who had been a friend for at least 15 years, say all that could be said on my behalf, and he did address the Court with his customary elegance and eloquence. In his speech in mitigation he said that I was affectionately referred to as "Uncle Eric" by most of the regular defendants, a form of address which I thought was confined to my overseas student friends.

When the mitigation had finished the Magistrate looked at me severely, and I think that the account of what he said that appeared in the *Daily Telegraph* next day was accurate, although frankly, I was too stunned by the proceedings to be quite sure.

> "Mr Davies told Mr Crowther: 'Your behaviour has given this Court grave cause for concern. You will be placed on probation for an indefinite period.'

'May I have a lady probation officer?' I ventured, looking meaningfully at Beverley Thatcher, the attractive Senior.

Roger ignored that request but invited me to sit, and, changing his tone, observed:

'For the past 21 years Eric Crowther has administered Justice in London with firmness, fairness, compassion, courtesy, understanding and humour.

'He has sparkled on the Bench. We will all miss him sorely.'"

Like John Dooley earlier that morning, I felt, after Roger's magnanimous remarks, that I had reason to be proud. The *Telegraph* was right when it recorded that for once I was at a loss for words.

A moment later – it was 10 to 11 by now – I was on the Bench of Court Number One at Horseferry Road with Anthony Maxwell standing shabby, shambling and dishevelled in front of me.

"Were you using threatening behaviour on the Piazza in front of Westminster Cathedral?" asked Miss Glenn, as if nothing had happened.

"Not Guilty," croaked Anthony Maxwell.

I was amazed. Mr Maxwell is an appalling, even dangerous, nuisance who appears before the Court for threatening behaviour or drunk and disorderly almost daily, but he invariably pleads guilty. I think that the shock of temporarily sharing a cell with me had affected what remained of his judgment, his situation being further aggravated by the alcohol, the signs of which had still been on him when we had just met, despite his arrest many hours earlier.

I have frequently seen Anthony Maxwell menacing shopkeepers in the Victoria area – even the ladies' hairdressers – with demands for money for the daily ration of lager on which he survives. On one occasion in the market of Strutton Ground he had a young German tourist up against the wall and holding up his clenched fist, he was threatening:

"You'll get this in your face if you don't give me your wallet!"

I lacked the courage to carry out a citizen's arrest, but I did intervene to warn him: "Mr Maxwell, I shall remember this when you make your daily appearance before me tomorrow."

"Sorry, Mr Crowther," he crumbled, "I didn't mean no harm," and his victim was able to escape.

Another tourist was less lucky, for I arrived just too late. As I walked along Victoria Street I saw this tall Swedish lady hand Mr Maxwell a coin from her purse and he seemed grateful. But a few seconds later he returned to deliver a savage kick to her leg, as a result of which she fell to the ground, while he shouted: "Take that, you bloody mean foreign bitch!"

Then, seeing me again, he shambled off.

"What did I do wrong?" she asked, as I picked her up. "He seemed so grateful at first."

"You had the misfortune to cross the path of Anthony Maxwell," I explained. "How much did you give him?"

"One of these," she replied, showing me a 20-pence piece.

"Ah, that explains it," I illuminated. "Mr Maxwell does not always see very well and at first he thought it was a pound."

I welcomed the abolition of the law against incorrigible rogues until I met Anthony Maxwell. When I saw him the next day after the Swedish incident I warned him that when he appeared before me in future I would normally give him the maximum sentence that the law permitted.

"Not Guilty!" I exclaimed with all the ferocity of the Magistrate Mr Fang who tried Oliver Twist. "That's a very unwise plea today if I may say so."

"Very well, guilty," Maxwell husked.

"That's better," I mollified. "What was he doing? Being Anthony Maxwell?"

"Precisely," rejoined the charming Crown Prosecutor, Miss Churiman, never an advocate to waste time.

I then passed to sentence the old reprobate from Belfast: "You will be discharged on condition that you keep sober and are of good behaviour for seven days."

I am writing this two days later, on Sunday September 24 on a flight to India, with Elke and her sister; I am going there to lecture for the British Council. I am sure that if Mr Maxwell was not back before the Court yesterday he will be there tomorrow. But I am hopeful that John

Dooley will not return at all. If I have saved him I feel that I have achieved something in the last 21 years.

On my penultimate day I sat an extra day to help Ronnie Bartle, who wanted to do something else then. I found myself in Court No. 1 at Bow Street, surely the most famous Magistrates' Courtroom in the world. Many notorious criminals have stood in the dock there. I myself was fined 30 shillings in that Courtroom for speeding by Sir Lawrence Dunne and £1 for having defective steering by Sir Robert Blundell, the latter informing me: "You are a menace to yourself and everybody else." He was to write me a charming letter of thanks when I had been sitting at Bow Street as a deputy in 1967: "Where would we be," he asked rhetorically in that letter, "without people with such a sense of duty to the public as you?" I decided not to remind him of the view of my character that he had expressed in his Court 12 years earlier.

Long before that, in 1947, when I was a costs clerk working for a dreary firm of solicitors in Lincoln's Inn Fields, I used to go into Bow Street on my free Saturday mornings (we worked every other Saturday in the solicitors' office) and watch Sir Lawrence and Sir Robert at work and think: "Maybe one day I will be sitting where you are sitting."

Well, I was, on September 21, 1989, and I decided to celebrate in a rather special way. In my impecunious days at the Bar, which coincided with the time when Roy was my clerk, I used to lunch at Mick's Cafe in Fleet Street. I always had the cheapest meal on the menu, which was steak pie, chips and baked beans, (Tips were not customary, a further advantage of Mick's). I had not been there since I changed to Q.E.B. with Robert as my clerk in 1962 – I rarely had time for lunch anyway in those busy Chambers – so I decided to return to Mick's from Bow Street after more than a quarter of a century. I was very relieved to find that it was still there, and that the cheapest meal on the menu was – steak pie, chips and baked beans. I decided to wash it down with a cup of tea and although I said rather firmly: "No milk, no sugar", both these commodities were inserted in copious quantities. The bill came to £1.65 which I suppose is just about consistent with inflation over the same period, but the cup of sickly sweet milky tea had gone up from only two (old) pence to five new ones. The food was as good as ever, but Mick's did seem just a bit scruffier. For the first time at Mick's I left a tip.

On my first day, August 1, 1968, my sister Eileen attended at South Western Magistrates' Court to hear me try a nasty case – my only trial that day – indecent assault on a small child which resulted in the defendant's receiving six months imprisonment. My clerk on that day was Donagh Gleeson, sensible, sophisticated, helpful and discreet. My wife Elke was with me on my last day, September 22, 1989, when in the afternoon my clerk was Donagh Gleeson, sensible, sophisticated, helpful and discreet – but still a deputy. What had gone wrong for him in the intervening years, I wonder? Whose path had he crossed? Certainly all the Stipendiaries and lay Magistrates at Horseferry Road thought very highly of him; yet he has had to sit back for two decades watching others get their own Courts, while promotion has not come his way. He has no idea that I am writing this, and he does not complain, but not everyone in the Inner London Magistrates' Court Service is fairly treated.

It is said that on his last day generous Big Jim Harmsworth gave everybody conditional discharges, and certainly I hoped to avoid sending anyone to prison during my final appearance. But it was not to be. A young man had been placed on probation the previous week by lay justices at Horseferry Road for selling cannabis at Victoria Coach Station – a too lenient disposal, in my opinion. Now, only a few days later, he was pleading guilty before me to selling cannabis at Victoria Station. I regard drugs, even soft ones, as the scourge of our young people. In vain did the duty solicitor seek to argue that "probation had not yet had time to work". I am afraid that his client finished up losing his liberty.

Otherwise once the cases of Crowther and Anthony Maxwell were out of the way, my last day was an unusually dull one. The Press had often said that I was noted for my "celebrated one-liners". One of the cases before me was that of a middle-aged West Indian of good character pleading guilty to driving with excess alcohol. He was only a little over the limit, but of course he had to lose his licence (and his job); many people do not realize this and erroneously think, as he did, that if they believed they were fit to drive they need not be disqualified. This is not the law: it is almost the only offence in sentencing for which Magistrates have no discretion; I wish we did have a discretion, as do Courts in Australia in respect of this type of offence, for mandatory disqualification can lead to a lot of hardship and even in some cases to injustice.

I recall at West London once a defendant, also of previous good character, who had been stopped because his rear light had gone out and he had been found to have 81 mg. of alcohol in his blood, the legal limit being 80. He seemed a very nice man, and I was really sorry for him.

"I'm afraid you'll have to be disqualified for a year," I announced sadly.

"Oh will I, really? That's awful," he exclaimed.

"Why, does your livelihood depend on your licence?"

"No, it's not that. It's my mother-in-law."

"I don't understand."

"Well, my mother-in-law reckons I can't do anything right, and my wife and I are supposed to be taking her on a three-week holiday in Scotland starting tomorrow – a sort of peace offering. She's always on at my wife that she should never have married me. I reckon this will mean the end of our marriage."

I pondered for a moment, then I said: "I'm finding it very difficult to determine the appropriate level of fine in this case. It's going to take me a long time to decide, so I shall adjourn the case for four weeks. In the meantime you can have your licence back, but you won't drink and drive, will you?"

"Gawd no, not with my mother-in-law around," he sighed. "But you're a proper gentleman."

"I advise you not to mention all this to your mother-in-law," was my parting admonition, but I often wondered during the intervening period how the three of them were getting on, north of the border.

The West Indian of my last day had no such matrimonial problems, but he was very repetitive, as litigants in person tend to be. The burden of what he was trying to say was that he was anaemic and his doctor had prescribed Guinness, that Guinness was much stronger than he had supposed and that he had had only one glass of the black liquid that day.

(This last statement I did not believe, although he was not much over the limit.) I was not very busy that day, so I decided to let him ramble on, but when he made these points for the fourth time I intervened with a rather feeble "one-liner", "I am afraid Guinness was not good for you," and I imposed a small fine and the mandatory year's disqualification.

Most days at Horseferry Road were much busier and livelier and more problematical than my last one. The previous week I had had a difficult, much more typical day, when three unusual and diverse problems had presented themselves.

One of these was the case of a 55-year-old taxi driver of excellent character, a singer and a TV personality, charged with indecent assault on a shy Indian girl who had been a passenger in his taxi one night. She alleged that, after a somewhat intimate conversation on the journey, he had got into the back of the cab with her as she fumbled in her bag to find the money for the fare, and fondled her breasts, which he strongly denied. There was no corroboration, in the legal sense of the term – she had been alone – but she was a convincing witness and I found it strange that during the ride he had (as he admitted) directed the conversation round to massage and sauna baths in the Finchley Road (many miles off the route). With reluctance I convicted him, realizing that this meant professional ruin for him.

Of the pleas (non-contested cases) several related, alas, to drugs. One was the case of a very bright university student who celebrated getting a First in his final examinations by buying £180 worth of cannabis and selling £11 worth of it to a friend. Were his brilliance, his excellent academic record, his good family background (his anxious parents had come all the way from Devon to support him) factors in mitigation or an aggravation of the crime? He came very near to an immediate prison sentence but finished up with 200 hours (almost the maximum) of community service and a £500 fine.

I earlier said that those who appear before Magistrates' Courts fall into three categories: the bad, the sad, and the mad. In another case that day the defendant bridged those last two categories. Her counsel described it as the saddest case with which he had ever had to deal. The

67-year-old spinster, a lady of good character, pleaded guilty to obtaining prescriptions for drugs by deception. She had been "hooked" on dexadrine for 43 years, and looked so ill that it was a marvel that she was still alive. She lived in Southwark, where she had her National Health doctor, but every week for seven months she went all the way to Richmond in Surrey to get prescriptions for dexadrine from a doctor there. In his own statement for the prosecution the doctor admitted prescribing for her 120 dexadrine tablets a week for 30 weeks. Then each time she got the drugs she telephoned the doctor to say that she had lost the prescription and on 16 occasions in those seven months, without any further inquiry, he just issued a further prescription, with the result that she was nearly dead when she came before me. I described the doctor as thoroughly incompetent, said that his conduct defied imagination, and that he should be reported to his professional association. I do not know whether he was, but the case received wide publicity, especially because, in placing the poor lady on probation for two years, I made the unusual condition that she should not visit that doctor in Richmond during that period.

The doctor told the local Press that the lady had assured him that she was not doing anything wrong and that he had done his best to try to help her with her particular problems. He added: "I was stunned by the Magistrate's criticism, since I was not invited to give evidence in my defence."

All that I can say about that is that when four weeks previously the defendant's counsel had made his strong condemnation of the doctor concerned, in remanding the lady on bail for a Social Inquiry Report, I had asked the Crown Prosecution Service to ensure the doctor's attendance on the next occasion, as I wanted from him an explanation of what I regarded as his unethical conduct. The representative of the C.P.S., a body on whose information one cannot, alas, always rely, assured me that the doctor had been notified and suggested that his name be called outside the Courtroom. When there was no answer the prosecutor read to me the doctor's sworn statement which constituted part of the prosecution case, and this supported entirely the defence counsel's contentions. How easy it is for good people to be led into trouble.

The reader will feel, I think, that my life has been studded with coincidences, starred with unexpected reunions, but I really do feel that, despite the size of the city of my birth, legal London is just a village.

I had a bus which I used for transporting my students of the Cromwell School of English to places of interest in and around London for three weeks during each year. For the other 49 weeks it reposed in the underground car park at Horseferry Road Magistrates' Court. With my retirement, I did not feel that I should keep it there any longer, and, having no garage, I did not want the expense of taxing and insuring it to keep it on the street, so I advertised it in September 1989 in *Exchange and Mart*, asking £1,300: "no offers".

I got only one reply: a telephone call at 7.45 a.m. on the day on which the advertisement appeared. "How's the bodywork?" asked the caller. "There's a dent in the back door where someone ran into it," I replied.

"Right, I'll come round with a cheque for £1,250 which I'll give you straight away, if I like it."

"The advert says £1,300 and no offers."

"Yes, and £50 off for the dent in the door."

"I took that into account when I fixed the price of £1,300 with no offers."

"You're a hard man," judged the caller. "Right, I'll have a cheque for £1,300 ready which I'll hand over if I like the motor. Who shall I make the cheque out to?"

"E. Crowther," I replied.

"You mean 'E' for 'Eric', like the Magistrate?" asked the caller.

"Yes. 'E' for 'Eric', just like the Magistrate," I said. "And the vehicle is available for inspection this afternoon at 5 o'clock at Horseferry Road Magistrates' Court."

Despite the shock that this must have caused him the would-be purchaser duly turned up with his father at Court that afternoon. "I remember you now," he said, "I used to appear at Thames Court in me young days. You gave me a chance in 1973. You put me on probation for three years for taking and driving away. I've been out of trouble ever since."

"That's more than you did for me," grumbled his father. "You gave me six months – twice!"

But they liked "the motor" and handed over the cheque for £1,300, and, despite their criminal records, and the tattoos all up Dad's brawny arms, I decided that I liked them and trusted them and I let them drive off in the minibus that night, before the cheque had been cleared. I did not regret it. Not only did the cheque not bounce, but a few days later I received through the post a quite elegant pair of gloves that I had inadvertently left in the vehicle. Some leopards do change their spots.

I had invited about 200 legal friends to my Farewell Party on the evening of September 21, 1989. Not all were able to come, of course, but there was a goodly crowd. Most who could not make it were kind enough to write letters, although I had marked the invitation cards "No need to R.S.V.P. Just come if you can".

One who both attended and wrote a letter was Barrington Black who, as a solicitor in the North of England, had defended the Yorkshire Ripper and was to become a much-liked Stipendiary colleague at Marylebone. Barry is noted for his razor-sharp wit. A good friend of ours, a lady, once attended his Court when he was hearing an important murder commital. "He's just 'ace,'" was her verdict on Barry.

Barry could usually be relied upon to enliven our Stipes' quarterly meetings, an extraordinary amount of time at which used to be occupied by the consideration of whether our spouses should be invited to our social gatherings. On one such occasion one faithful Magistrate proposed that wives should come to our annual cocktail party, always well arranged by Ronnie Bartle at the Garrick. One of the few bachelor Stipes suggested an amendment: "I propose," he said, "that wives *and* girlfriends should be invited."

"That's going to create a difficulty," remarked Barry pensively, "because my wife doesn't know my girlfriend."

This was a more good-natured observation than that made some years earlier by a former colleague, now deceased, whose love of his fellow creatures seemed to be limited to policemen and dogs. Her Majesty the Queen and Prince Philip had accepted our invitation to our 250th anniversary dinner, and someone again proposed that our wives should be with us.

"What about the Stipe who hasn't got a wife?" asked a celibate Magistrate, plaintively.

"And what about the Stipe who has got a wife and can't stand the sight of her?" demanded this disgruntled old battle-cruiser.

Another more recent stipes' meeting was dragging drearily on into the evening and I wanted to get away to my Scottish Dancing. "Excuse me," I said to the Chief as I got up to leave. "I have to go to one of my extra-mural activities."

"Does he mean that he's actually going to sit in Court?" Barry interposed.

Anyway, after that introduction of Barry, it was inevitable that his farewell letter to me would make me laugh. It read as follows:

> "It was, perhaps, my own ill-chosen words that caused the tears to spring into the eyes of those small children, who had never even met the man.
>
> 'Eric Crowther is on his way out' I had said. The reaction was immediate. 'How could this be happening to a man so young?' they asked, 'a man who had not a grey head amongst his hair.'
>
> Their spoken thoughts came tumbling out, 'A Magistrate who puts so much thought, devotion, compassion, sincerity, judicial analysis, depth of understanding, and above all experience, into his – Scottish Dancing.'"

Barry's colleague at Marylebone, Quentin, "the Hat", Campbell, was equally witty. At about the time of my retirement I received from Turkey a postcard depicting a voluptuous belly-dancer, written in bad German. It began "Lieber Herr Crowther (in meinem Hertz, du beliebter Erich)" and finished threatening that in a week the writer was coming to London to find me – "meine Liebeshoffnung" – and it was signed "Deine Fatima". In my efforts to discover who had sent this I commented to my colleagues: "I wrote about a belly-dancer called Fatima in my earlier book, *Last in the List*, so it must be somebody who has read that book."

"That limits the field considerably," declared Quentin. "Are you sure you didn't write the card yourself?"

Well, as this is the last book that I intend to write (I want to read a lot more in the future) I pondered a long time on a good title and an appropriate ending. As recited in Chapter I a lady defendant thoughtfully supplied me with the former, but I have to depend on my own recollections and research for the latter.

I have always liked the ending of "Abou Ben Adhem" by Leigh Hunt: "Write me as one who loved his fellow men"; but it is so well known as almost to be commonplace. I have heard Lord Denning recite to Commonwealth Magistrates an American poem:-

"Four things a man must learn to do
If he would make his record true:
To think, without confusion, clearly;
To act from honest motives, purely;
To love his fellow men sincerely;
And trust in God and Heaven, surely."

But the printed page cannot bring to life Denning's delightful Hampshire brogue. I liked, too, the motto of a public school: "He who has faith conquers all." But it was not my public school, so it would seem a bit disloyal to finish with that line.

Then, quite by chance, I came across some lines by W.H. Auden which appealed to me greatly, but then I mislaid them. A thorough search proving unavailing, I resolved to write to Sir Stephen Spender, c/o the B.B.C., to enlist his assistance, as I knew him to have been a close friend of Auden, and Spender had attended my school (University College School), albeit somewhat earlier than I. I asked him if he could think of anything Auden had written that was suitable to my situation.

Sir Stephen wrote me an exceedingly kind letter, but was unable to help, so I started reading Auden, who wrote a terrific lot. Although I did not admire his life-style, I came to like some of his poetry very much, and was tempted to finish with this bit of doggerel:-

"Law, says the Judge, as he looks down his nose,
Speaking clearly and most severely,
Law is, as I've told you before,
Law is, as you know, I suppose,
Law is, but let me explain it once more,
Law is – The Law;"

or this:-

"At last the secret is out, as it always must come to an end,
The delicious story is right to tell to the intimate friend;
Over the tea-cups and in the square the tongue has its desire;"

But then there is bathos as the quartet finishes with the hackneyed final line, the last five cruel words of which I do not believe to be true:-

"Still waters run deep, my dear, there's never smoke without fire;"

until, surprise, surprise, I found tucked away in my wallet, just after my farewell party attended by so many good friends, the original passage of Auden that I had liked and lost and with which I now make my literary exit:-

"Among those I like and admire I can find no common denominator, but among those whom I love, I can: all of them make me laugh."

INDEX